Romeo and Juliet

A PRACTICAL GUIDE FOR TEACHING SHAKESPEARE
IN THE MIDDLE GRADE CLASSROOM

Retold by Alain Chirinian

Illustrated by Robin DeWitt & Patricia Grush

Project Director: Mina McMullin

Senior Editor: Christine Hood

Inside and Cover Design: Rita Hudson

Cover Illustration: Robin DeWitt

© 1997 Good Apple. All rights reserved. Printed in the United States of America.

GOOD APPLE
A Division of Frank Schaffer Publications
23740 Hawthorne Blvd.
Torrance, CA 90505

Notice! Pages may be reproduced for classroom or home use only, not for commercial resale. No part of this publication may be reproduced for storage in a retrieval system, or transmitted in any form or by any means—electronic, mechanical, recording, etc.—without the prior written permission of the publisher. Reproduction of these materials for an entire school system is strictly prohibited.

Contents

Introduction 4

The Life and Times of William Shakespeare 5

The Elizabethan Stage 7

About *Romeo and Juliet* 9

Romeo and Juliet Summary 10

Cast of Characters 16

Romeo and Juliet 17

Vocabulary 43

Introducing Drama 45

Elements of a Story 46

The Language of Shakespeare 47

Let's Put on a Play! 48

Journal/Discussion Topics 51

Extension Activities 55

References 64

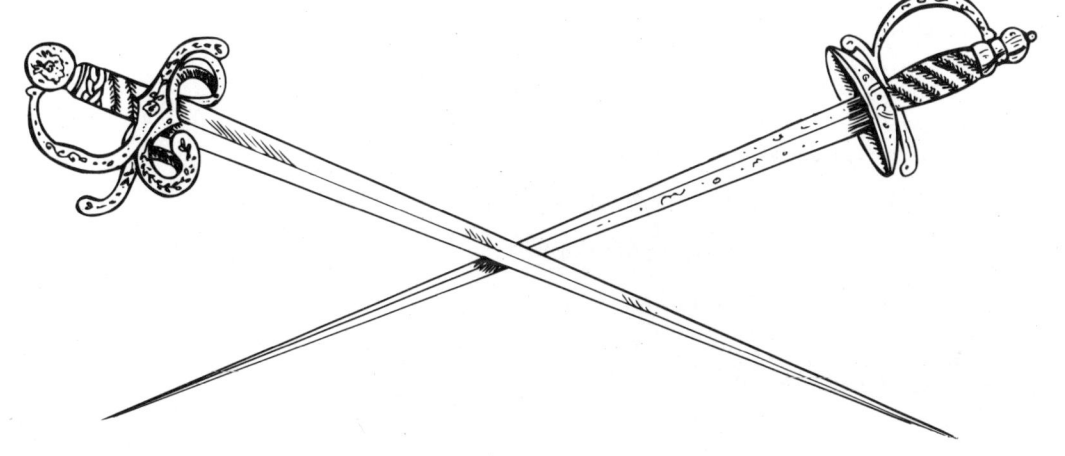

Introduction

If you asked 100 people to name the greatest writer in history, most of them would probably say, *William Shakespeare*. Shakespeare, a cultural icon of the English-speaking world, has been revered throughout history for his extraordinary skill with language; his unforgettable characters; and his wonderful, many-faceted stories. Some people have been led to believe that Shakespeare is difficult to understand or just not relevant to today's world. Unfortunately, many students' first exposure to Shakespeare may be sitting in a classroom passively listening to the teacher lecture or analyzing passages that seem to have no meaning or relevance to their lives. Studying Shakespeare should not be a "passive" experience; rather, it should be exciting, stimulating, and most of all, fun! It is for this reason that this book was created.

When students are drawn into the humanity of Shakespeare's work, they see how it relates to their lives and the world around them. His themes are central to the struggles and triumphs of humankind; his characters highlight the strength, passion, and joy of humanity as well as its darker, more malevolent side. Although the settings of his stories are in faraway times and places, they deal with contemporary topics. Shakespeare wrote of people in the depths of despair, the throes of comic madness, diabolical plotting, scheming, wooing, and "lovemaking." This may sound like the stuff of soap operas, movies, or TV sitcoms, but that is exactly why students will relate to Shakespeare—a writer for all ages.

In order for students to truly enjoy and appreciate Shakespeare, they shouldn't just read his work, but rather, "experience" it. Before beginning a play study, introduce Shakespeare as a person. Where was he born? What do we know about his life? his family? What was England like during Shakespeare's time? Were his plays as popular then as they are today? What was the life of an actor and playwright like in Elizabethan England? Answering these and other questions for students gives them a personal and historical perspective on Shakespeare and the Elizabethan stage, complementing their overall understanding and enjoyment of his plays.

This book contains a simple summary and an edited version of the play *Romeo and Juliet*, in which some language has been simplified for easier student understanding. It also provides suggestions for performing the play; a comprehensive vocabulary list; journal/discussion topics; and a myriad of activities that draw students into the plot, characters, and meaning of the story. These activities will help develop children's imaginations; language and critical-thinking skills; and creative expression through writing, dramatic presentation, and art.

If students' first encounter with Shakespeare is a positive one, they will be "turned on" to future experiences. Learning that "old" doesn't necessarily mean "old-fashioned" opens not only Shakespeare's world to students, but also that of other classic writers and artists.

The Life and Times of William Shakespeare

Shakespeare's plays do not reveal much about him as a person. Since the plots are so varied and deal with a myriad of social and political issues, Shakespeare's actual views remain elusive and mysterious.

Shakespeare's birthday is recognized as April 23, 1564. He was born in the small English town of Stratford-upon-Avon. The town's name developed because Stratford was nestled next to the River Avon. Shakespeare's father, John, was a successful Stratford glove maker who dealt in leather goods; and his mother, Mary Arden, came from a wealthy Catholic family.

Not much is known about Shakespeare until his marriage to Anne Hathaway in 1582. He was 18 and she was 26. During their marriage, they had three children—Susanna, born in 1583, and the twins Judith and Hamnet, born in 1585.

From 1585 to 1592, no official records exist on Shakespeare. But by the age of 28, he had moved to London and become an actor with a small company of players. Even as he became a successful playwright, he continued to act in his own and others' plays. Between 1589 and 1594, Shakespeare's first plays, *Henry VI*, *Titus Andronicus*, and *The Comedy of Errors*, were a huge success in the London theatre circuit. Shakespeare soon made a name for himself and attained instant popularity.

London was a very exciting place during Shakespeare's time. Elizabeth I was queen when he began his career. English ships ruled the seas, and English explorers were claiming territories as far away as America and the Far East. Shakespeare incorporated much of the excitement, mystery, and adventure of this time period into his work. Unfortunately, in the early 1590s, the plague in London led to the closing of all the theatres. During this time, Shakespeare began writing poetry, including his famous sonnets. This poetry demonstrates Shakespeare's true artistic skill with verse.

When the theatres reopened around 1594, Shakespeare helped form the acting company known as the Lord Chamberlain's Men. For the next ten years, it was London's most popular acting company. The company also started its own theater—the Globe—and Shakespeare became the primary shareholder. The Globe became a popular entertainment spot for both commoners and wealthy aristocrats.

Shakespeare's greatest writing occurred between 1599 and 1608. During this time, he wrote such popular plays as *Twelfth Night*, *Hamlet*, *Macbeth*, and *Othello*. In 1603, with the succession of James I, Shakespeare's company received a royal patent, and they changed their name to the King's Men. They were then able to perform at the royal court several times a year.

Between 1610 and 1611, Shakespeare retired to his home in Stratford. Here he collaborated with John Fletcher on three more plays—*Henry VIII*, *The Two Noble Kinsmen*, and *Cardenio*.

In 1616, Shakespeare died at the young age of 52. Records show that he was buried on April 25, so it's assumed he died on April 23, two days earlier. This date has been suspect since it is also his birthday. No one knows how Shakespeare died, so his death remains shrouded in mystery. Over 20 possible causes of death have been speculated, including writer's cramp, too much alcohol, and murder.

Regardless of what brought Shakespeare to his demise, his incredible life left humankind a prolific treasure in his writings. Shakespeare wrote 37 plays, 154 sonnets, and two narrative poems. His plays fall into three categories: histories such as *Richard III* and *Henry V*, tragedies such as *Macbeth* and *Othello*, and comedies such as *Twelfth Night* and *As You Like It*.

Shakespeare's deep understanding of human nature and his incredible talent for making characters realistic and human make his work uniquely great. Most aspects of human nature haven't changed much from Elizabethan England. One may even find something of him- or herself or a friend in one of Shakespeare's characters. Much as they did in Elizabethan England, these plays can still move audiences to tears or make them roar with laughter. It is these timeless qualities that keep Shakespeare at the top of the literary and theatrical world.

The Elizabethan Stage

Theatre was an entirely different experience for the Elizabethans than it is for audiences today. The stage was round, so the audience was highly involved in the performance. Actors sometimes spoke to the audience through soliloquies and asides, and audience members often answered back. Elizabethan theatregoers yelled, laughed, taunted, talked, and ate throughout the performance.

During the Elizabethan period, politicians and clergy were opposed to the theatre, claiming it was a dangerous diversion from religion. So, playhouses were banned in London's city proper and forced out to the suburbs in an area known as Southwark. In this "theatre district," patrons could choose between nine different theatres. Strewn among the theatres were pubs, taverns, and bawdy houses as well as pickpockets and thieves, which only added to the theatre's already bad reputation.

When a play was about to begin, it was a announced with a raised flag and a trumpeted fanfare. The flag indicated the theme of that day's play—black for tragedy, white for comedy, and red for history. When patrons entered a theatre for a performance, they placed their admission money in a box (or "box office"). They could sit in the "galleries" on wooden benches, on cushions in front of the stage, on the stage itself (for more money), or stand in back with the crowd. The general "mob scene" of the crowd (known as "groundlings") created quite a spectacle. Since few Elizabethans bathed, the theatres smelled of sweat, beer, and garlic. It's no wonder the groundlings were also referred to as

"penny stinkards." Vendors sold beer, fruit, and nuts, and in the often tumultuous, rowdy atmosphere of a play, these snacks would sometimes be thrown at the actors onstage.

Like all other playhouses, Shakespeare's Globe was under the patronage of a nobleman. This patronage provided protection from the Puritans as well as additional financial backing. Shakespeare's company was originally "attached" to Lord Chamberlain, and later to James I, becoming the most prestigious theatre company in London.

Shakespeare wrote specifically for his stage in the Globe. Often referred to as a "wooden O," the Globe may have had as many as 20 sides to provide its circular appearance. The theatre was open to the outside and could hold close to 3,000 people. The stage consisted of three tiers—"heaven," "earth," and "hell." A trapdoor in the main stage, or "earth," was used to raise and lower actors and props into and out of "hell." A canopy over the stage was painted with golden stars to represent the "heavens." Often, pulleys and ropes lowered or "whisked" actors up to and from "heaven." A hut on top of the canopy housed props for sound effects such as thunder and cannon fire. Audiences hooted and hollered with delight when such special stage and sound effects were used.

Unlike plays and movies today, scenery and props were limited. To let the audience know what time of day it was or what the weather was like, it was described with an actor's words. For example, when Romeo and Juliet awaken in her chamber, we know it is morning when Romeo says, "It was the lark, the herald of the morn . . . Look, love, what envious streaks do lace the severing clouds in yonder east." Actors also wore elaborate, gawdy costumes and makeup, which were considered sinful by the clergy.

During this time, women were not allowed to act on the public stage, so young boys played the female roles. That is one reason why there are so few women characters in Shakespeare's plays. Not being able to rely on "traditional" feminine beauty for his female characters, Shakespeare created those with amazing intelligence and wit.

Theatres put on a great variety of plays every season. In six months, one company might give about 150 performances of 25 to 30 different plays. Given the quick turnover, rehearsal time was extremely short. Actors only had about a week to learn their parts—up to 800 lines a day for leading roles!

Unfortunately, Shakespeare's revered Globe Theatre burned down in 1613 during a performance of *Henry VIII*. A prop cannon exploded and set the theatre aflame. The theatre was eventually rebuilt, but in 1642, the Puritans finally got their way. The English Parliament passed an ordinance shutting down all theatres, and as a result, the Globe was destroyed in 1644.

About *Romeo and Juliet*

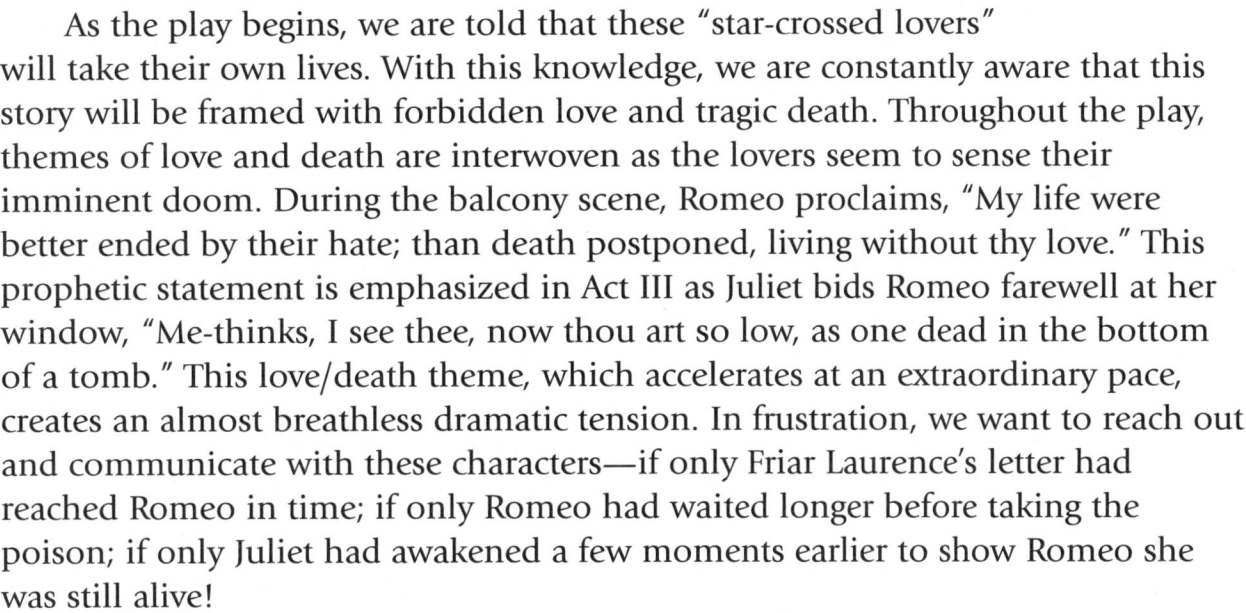

"For now, these hot days, is the mad blood stirring." These words, spoken by Romeo's friend, Benvolio, describes the atmosphere behind this tragic love story. The streets are hot, the feud bitter, the action quick. In four short days, Romeo and Juliet meet, fall in love, marry, and die. This incredibly passionate and sympathetic story captures the intensity and exhilaration of first love.

As the play begins, we are told that these "star-crossed lovers" will take their own lives. With this knowledge, we are constantly aware that this story will be framed with forbidden love and tragic death. Throughout the play, themes of love and death are interwoven as the lovers seem to sense their imminent doom. During the balcony scene, Romeo proclaims, "My life were better ended by their hate; than death postponed, living without thy love." This prophetic statement is emphasized in Act III as Juliet bids Romeo farewell at her window, "Me-thinks, I see thee, now thou art so low, as one dead in the bottom of a tomb." This love/death theme, which accelerates at an extraordinary pace, creates an almost breathless dramatic tension. In frustration, we want to reach out and communicate with these characters—if only Friar Laurence's letter had reached Romeo in time; if only Romeo had waited longer before taking the poison; if only Juliet had awakened a few moments earlier to show Romeo she was still alive!

Most Shakespearean tragedies are those with characters possessing a "fatal flaw," but this romantic tragedy is one of circumstance and rashness. The lovers are victims of bad timing, misunderstandings, and mistakes. The seemingly thoughtless, impulsive actions of many characters in this play lead not only to Romeo's and Juliet's deaths, but also to those of Tybalt, Mercutio, and Paris. Their deaths teach us a valuable lesson about the futility of feuding and violence.

Romeo and Juliet, first performed in 1594, became an instant success. It was popular in its own right, but also because it was controversial, encouraging marriage for love rather than by parental choice. This play remains one of the most enduring love stories ever told. Today it continues to be one of Shakespeare's most performed and well-loved plays.

Romeo and Juliet
Summary

Once, in the Italian city of Verona, there lived two feuding families—the Montagues and the Capulets. They had hated each other for many years, each generation passing the feud on to the next. We enter this story on a hot, sunny afternoon after many years of fighting, feuding, and bitterness.

❦ ACT ONE ❦

Several Montagues and their friends are enjoying themselves in the town marketplace. Delicious smells from roasting meat and fresh-baked bread fill the air. Vendors call out to the young men as they wander through the marketplace, joking and laughing under the hot sun. Across the square, several Capulets are enjoying themselves as well. Walking toward the center of the square, they spot the Montagues. After much cajoling and name-calling, bitterness fills the air. A scuffle begins, and Benvolio tries to break it up. Tybalt, throwing out more insults, draws his sword and challenges a fight. Swords drawn, the two groups rush toward each other. Children are whisked away by frightened parents, and carts of food are pushed out of the way. Metal upon metal screeches as swords clash, and blood flows to the ground. Several Montagues and Capulets are seriously hurt.

During the fight, Lord and Lady Capulet and Lord and Lady Montague arrive on the scene. Just as the Lords are about to fight, the prince of Verona appears followed by six armed guards. As the prince and his men enter the square, the fighting immediately stops. "You there, Montague!" commands the prince, pointing. "And you, Capulet! This senseless violence will end now. Upon penalty of death, I bid you to stop all such displays when in my kingdom!"

Both Capulets and Montagues consider themselves fortunate not to have been punished more severely by the prince. As they turn to go home, Lady Montague asks Benvolio to talk with her son, Romeo, for he seemed depressed.

Moments later, Romeo enters the square, looking sad and dejected. Benvolio asks Romeo why he's sad, and Romeo tells Benvolio that he is in love with the beautiful Rosaline, who has not returned his affections. As they wander the streets, Romeo and Benvolio run into Sampson, a servant of the Capulet family. Sampson is holding a list of invitations to a party. Sampson tells them they are invited to a party at the Capulets that evening as long as they aren't Montagues. When Romeo discovers Rosaline will be there, he decides to go.

Meanwhile, Juliet, Lord and Lady Capulet's only daughter, speaks with her mother and nurse in her bedroom. Lady Capulet asks her daughter how she feels about marriage and expresses concern that Juliet has not yet married. Most of Juliet's cousins already have children of their own, and they are younger than she. Lady Capulet tells Juliet about Paris, "a man of honor and reputation, with noble blood." He will be at the party that evening, and Lady Capulet encourages Juliet to meet him to see if he would be an agreeable husband. Juliet agrees to the meeting.

Romeo and his friends Mercutio and Benvolio make their way to the Capulet masquerade party. They are wearing masks so no one will recognize them as Montagues. Almost immediately after they arrive, Romeo notices the beautiful Juliet as she dances to the enchanting music. Several young men are waiting their turn to dance with her.

From a nearby balcony, Juliet's cousin Tybalt recognizes Romeo below among the guests. He is shocked that a Montague would dare enter the house of Capulet. Tybalt draws his sword, ready to attack Romeo. But his uncle, Lord Capulet, stops him, not wanting violence to spoil the party.

Juliet's heart flutters when Romeo asks her to dance. As they dance, they cannot take their eyes off each other. The music and people around them melt away, and nothing else in the world seems to matter. Romeo and Juliet soon realize they are falling in love. Neither of them has ever felt this way before. When they find a moment alone, they embrace and kiss passionately. Later, as Romeo and his friends leave the party, Romeo asks a servant the identity of the beautiful young woman with whom he was dancing. He is devastated with the news that Juliet is the only daughter of his family's bitter enemy.

⚜ ACT TWO ⚜

Outside the Capulet home, Mercutio and Benvolio search for Romeo. Figuring he has gone home to bed, the two depart. They don't realize Romeo is hiding from them. He feels compelled to stay near the Capulet home. "Can I go forward when my heart is here?" Romeo thinks to himself. He remains hidden behind shrubs near the house.

In the light of the full moon, Juliet suddenly appears on the balcony outside her bedroom. Romeo excitedly crawls under a tree near the window, carefully remaining hidden, and gazes at the lovely Juliet above him. Juliet believes herself to be alone and gazes out into the moonlit garden. She calls out Romeo's name, and to her surprise, he answers her from below. He climbs up onto the balcony. And though their families are enemies, Romeo and Juliet pledge their love to each other. Juliet tells him if he intends to marry her to send word the following day. She reluctantly encourages him to go because she is afraid of what might happen if someone finds him there. With one last kiss, Romeo climbs down the balcony into the night.

Romeo wanders through the woods all night, his mind full with thoughts of his beloved. At daylight, he meets Friar Laurence, who is collecting flowers and herbs. The friar can tell Romeo has not slept all night and asks him to sit down. Romeo tells him his story of finding true love among his enemies, and asks the friar to marry he and Juliet that afternoon. Friar Laurence always thought the feud between the Capulets and Montagues needless and tragic, and believes a marriage between the two families may lead to an end to the violence. He agrees to perform the marriage ceremony for Romeo and Juliet that afternoon.

Later that morning, Romeo finds Juliet's nurse and tells her his plan to marry Juliet in secret. The nurse agrees to give Juliet the good news when they're alone. That afternoon, Romeo and Juliet meet at Friar Laurence's cell and are secretly married.

ACT THREE

That same afternoon, Benvolio and Mercutio meet in the marketplace. Several Capulets, including Tybalt, are also present. Tybalt is still upset about Romeo appearing at the Capulets' party, and he exchanges insults with Mercutio.

Unaware of Tybalt's anger, Romeo approaches them from across the square. Tybalt challenges Romeo to fight, not knowing they are now related by marriage. Romeo, speaking words of love and peace to Tybalt, now his cousin, has no wish to fight. As Tybalt continues to mock Romeo, Mercutio becomes increasingly incensed with Tybalt's insults to his friend. To defend Romeo's honor, Mercutio draws his sword on Tybalt. Romeo tries to stop the fight by reminding them of the prince's order for peace, but they do not listen. In desperation, Romeo tries to separate the fighting men by grabbing hold of Mercutio. While Mercutio struggles with Romeo, Tybalt stabs him. Mercutio collapses and dies in Romeo's arms. Blind with pain and rage, Romeo picks up his dead friend's sword and begins fighting viciously with Tybalt. People clear the marketplace in fear, and Romeo stabs Tybalt, killing him. Horrified with what he has done, Romeo runs away.

When word of Mercutio's and Tybalt's deaths reach the prince, he gathers the Montagues and Capulets together. The prince had ordered the death of any Capulet or Montague who fought in Verona, and Lady Capulet asks him to carry out his word by executing Romeo. Lord Montague pleads with the prince to have mercy on his son, since Tybalt started the fight and killed Mercutio. The prince immediately renders punishment—Romeo will be banished from Verona, not to return on penalty of death.

Meanwhile, happily unaware of what has happened, Juliet prepares for her wedding night with Romeo. Suddenly, her nurse arrives. "Tybalt is dead!" the nurse cries. "And Romeo is banished for killing him!" Juliet is consumed with grief. Her cousin dead! And killed by her own husband! Juliet is somewhat comforted knowing Romeo only killed Tybalt in self defense, and her loyalty to her husband prevails. Seeing Juliet so distraught, the nurse offers to find Romeo so he can see her before he is forced to leave Verona.

Romeo hides in Friar Laurence's cell while waiting for news of the prince's punishment, wondering if it will be a death sentence. Soon the friar arrives and tells Romeo he is only banished for killing Tybalt. "I would rather be killed," Romeo exclaims, knowing this means he will never see Juliet and fair Verona again. Juliet's nurse finds Romeo in Friar Laurence's cell and tells him that Juliet needs to see him before he leaves. She gives him a ring from Juliet, and Romeo leaves immediately to see her.

When Romeo finds Juliet, she is happy to see him, yet afraid for their future together. Romeo knows he must leave or be put to death. The couple talk together throughout the night about what they will do. When daylight comes, they sorrowfully part. Juliet reaches out to Romeo as he climbs down the balcony into the misty morning. "Will we ever meet again?" she asks. "I have no doubt," Romeo answers, reassuring her.

Lord and Lady Capulet, unaware of their daughter's marriage to Romeo, inform Juliet that she will marry Paris, the young nobleman, in two days. Juliet is devastated. Thinking Juliet grieves over her cousin's death, Lady Capulet suggests that the marriage will cheer her up. To her mother's surprise, Juliet proclaims she would rather die than marry Paris, and pleads for sympathy.

When Lord Capulet hears this news, he is beside himself with anger. He tells Juliet he will never see or speak to her again if she refuses to marry Paris. He leaves Juliet weeping in her chamber. Juliet turns to her nurse for help, but the nurse tells her that with Romeo being banished, she should go ahead and marry Paris. Juliet feels betrayed and vows never to confide in her nurse again. She decides to go see Friar Laurence as a last resort, hoping he can help her.

⚜ ACT FOUR ⚜

Juliet cries as she tells Friar Laurence what has happened. The friar sympathizes with the young girl and comes up with a plan that will allow her to be with Romeo. He tells Juliet to return home and agree to marry Paris, and then hands her a vial of liquid to drink the night before her wedding. The liquid will cause her to fall into a deep sleep and appear dead for 42 hours. Meanwhile, he will send word to Romeo that Juliet is not actually dead, but waiting to leave the city with him. Brimming with gratitude, Juliet thanks the friar and returns home.

Once home, Juliet tells her parents she has changed her mind and will indeed marry the man they have chosen for her. Lord Capulet is happy that his daughter has finally come to her senses. He knows Paris will be a good husband and the two will find happiness together.

The night before the wedding, it seems to Juliet that her mother and nurse will never leave her alone! They talk for what seems an eternity about plans for the next day's wedding. Juliet plays along, pretending to be interested in what they say just so they will leave her to herself. Finally, Juliet bids them good-night and is left alone in her room. "Farewell," Juliet whispers as they close the door, "I hope we will meet again." She looks at the vial Friar Laurence gave her and hesitates. What if she never wakes up? What if she wakes up too early in the family tomb surrounded by the dead? Juliet realizes she must trust the friar and believe his plan will succeed. "Romeo, I drink this to thee," she says, swallowing the bitter liquid.

The next morning, the Capulet household is brimming with happiness. Food is being prepared, decorations hung, and presents delivered. The nurse goes to Juliet's room to awaken her. There she finds Juliet sprawled across her bed, cold and pale, showing no signs of life. Screaming, the nurse calls to Lord and Lady Capulet. There will be no wedding that day. Instead, the Capulets prepare for the funeral of their only daughter.

⚜ ACT FIVE ⚜

In the meantime, Friar Laurence sends a message to Romeo, informing him of the plan. The message tells Romeo to return to Verona at once so he can be there when Juliet wakes up. Then he and Juliet can leave Verona together and live as husband and wife in exile. But unknown to Friar Laurence, the messenger has been detained in Verona, sealed inside a sick house. Therefore, he has been unable to proceed to Mantua with Friar Laurence's letter.

Now outside Verona, Romeo hears instead the news of Juliet's death from Balthasar, his faithful servant. Romeo, at first disbelieving and then stricken with grief, decides the only thing he can do is join his true love in death. He finds his way to an apothecary to purchase poison. Selling poison is against the law, but Romeo offers the poor apothecary lots of money to persuade him to sell the poison. Romeo then makes his way to the Capulet vault where all the Capulets are buried. There he hopes to find his beloved.

When Friar Lawrence hears that Romeo never received his letter, he runs from his cell toward the Capulet vault. He hopes to find Romeo and tell him the truth before he can see Juliet, supposedly dead.

In the Capulet vault, Tybalt and Juliet lie next to each other. Paris is there, mourning the loss of the woman he wished to marry. Suddenly, Paris hears someone entering the tomb. He hides in the shadows and watches as Romeo enters. Outraged, Paris steps into the light and challenges Romeo to a duel. At first, Romeo begs Paris not to fight, but when Paris insists he will kill him, Romeo draws his sword. The two men fight between the funeral beds of Juliet and Tybalt, until Romeo overcomes and kills Paris.

Romeo realizes he has now killed two people, and there before him is his Juliet, his true love and wife, lying dead. Seeing no reason to live a minute longer, he takes out the poison and drinks it. "Here's to my love," he tells the sleeping Juliet. Romeo struggles to give Juliet one last kiss, and then he dies.

Just moments too late, Friar Laurence arrives at the Capulet vault. Before him he sees the two new corpses of Paris and Romeo. As the friar mourns, Juliet begins to wake up. The friar fears what she will do when she sees Romeo's dead body. Juliet wakes up happy, knowing the friar's plan has worked. She can't wait to see her Romeo again and live happily with him for the rest of her life. Friar Laurence watches in agony as Juliet notices Romeo lying lifeless on the ground next to her. Nearby is the dead body of Paris. Juliet cries out and kneels next to her husband.

Suddenly, Friar Lawrence hears the sound of approaching footsteps. He pleads with Juliet to leave the tomb with him and runs out, assuming she follows. Instead, Juliet stays next to Romeo. She takes the vial from Romeo's hand, but finds it empty. She then kisses Romeo's lips, hoping there is some poison remaining there, and finds none. Finally, hearing the footsteps coming closer, Juliet desperately pulls Romeo's dagger from its sheath. "O happy dagger!" she cries, stabbing herself, "Let me die!"

The prince of Verona and his attendants soon enter the vault. He is joined by Lord Montague and Lord and Lady Capulet. Inside, they find the lifeless bodies of Paris, Romeo, and Juliet. Lord Montague already mourns for his wife, who died upon hearing of Romeo's banishment. Now his only son is dead as well.

Feeling partially responsible for the tragedy, Friar Laurence returns to the vault and explains the entire story to the prince. The prince, angered by the senseless violence, cries, "Capulet! Montague! See what punishment results from your hate. Heaven has killed your joys with love!" He asks the families to end their feud to prevent further devastation. Grief-stricken, the Capulets and Montagues finally realize what ends their fighting has wrought. They decide to end their feud and vow to cherish the memories of their children, never forgetting the lesson they have learned—that violence can only result in tragedy.

CAST OF CHARACTERS

Lord and Lady Montague aristocrats who are feuding with the Capulets

Lord and Lady Capulet aristocrats who are feuding with the Montagues

Romeo son of Lord and Lady Montague

Juliet daughter of Lord and Lady Capulet

Mercutio and Benvolio friends of Romeo and sworn enemies of the Capulets

Tybalt quick-tempered nephew of Lady Capulet

Nurse Juliet's nanny and companion

Prince Escalus prince of Verona

Paris a young nobleman

Friar Laurence a Franciscan monk and Juliet's religious advisor

Sampson and Gregory the Capulets' servants

Balthasar Romeo's servant

Apothecary a seller of medicine

Friar John a Franciscan monk

A servant of the Capulets

Citizens of Verona, including family members and friends of the Capulets and Montagues

Officers to the prince

SETTING

The story takes place in Verona, Italy, after many years of petty, interfamily feuding between the Capulets, the Montagues, and their friends.

Romeo and Juliet

Prologue

Chorus Two households, both alike in dignity,
In fair Verona, where we lay our scene,
From ancient grudge break to new mutiny,
Where civil blood makes civil hands unclean.
From forth the fatal families of these two foes
A pair of star-crossed lovers take their life;
Whose misadventured piteous overthrows
Do with their death bury their parents' strife.

ACT ONE

SCENE ONE *Verona, Italy. A marketplace filled with sounds and smells of people and animals, things being bought and sold, colorful flags waving, and music playing. Three young Capulet men are admiring fresh fruits and vegetables when they encounter several Montagues. Immediately, they begin to mock each other, then argue. They draw their swords and begin fighting. Benvolio forces himself between the fighting men, trying to stop them.*

Benvolio Part, fools! Put up your swords; you know not what you do!

Enter Tybalt from across the square.

Tybalt Turn thee, Benvolio, and look upon thy death!

Benvolio I only try to stop these men from fighting. Help me keep the peace.

Tybalt *(laughing)* What, drawn sword and talk of peace! I hate that word, as I hate all Montagues, and thee!

The men begin to fight again. Several on both sides are hurt. Enter Prince Escalus and his officers.

Prince Escalus Rebellious subjects, enemies of peace, throw your mistempered weapons to the ground!

Fearing the prince, the men immediately stop fighting and drop their swords.

Prince Escalus If you ever disturb our streets again, your lives shall be the cost! You, Capulet, come with me. And you, Montague, come this afternoon to learn more of my displeasure. Now, all of you, depart this place.

Carrying their wounded, the men leave without looking back. Benvolio remains behind. Enter Romeo, looking sad and dejected.

Benvolio Good morrow, cousin.

Romeo *(sighing deeply)* Is the day so young?

Benvolio What sadness lengthens Romeo's hours?

Romeo I cannot stop thinking of Rosaline. I have told her of my love, but she has refused my affections. It is as if I am shut in prison and kept without food.

Benvolio Tut, man! One fire burns out another. Take some new infection to thine eye, and the rank poison of the old will die.

Enter Sampson, carrying a piece of paper. It is a list of names of people invited to a masquerade party at the Capulets' that evening.

Sampson Good morrow, friends. There is a masque tonight.

Romeo *(taking the list from Sampson's hand, and reading it)* A masque? Tonight? Whither should they come?

Sampson To my master's house, sir. My master is the great rich Capulet. You and your friends are invited if you be not of the house of Montagues. Come and dine, dance, and crush a cup of wine. Rest you merry!

Exit Sampson, with the list.

Benvolio At this masque will sup the fair Rosaline, whom you love, with all the admired beauties of Verona. Go thither, and compare her face with some that I shall show, and I will make thee think thy swan a crow.

Romeo One fairer than my love? The all-seeing sun never saw her match, since first the world began. Very well, then. Let us attend the masque. Our faces shall be covered, so none will be the wiser. Let us meet at sunset.

SCENE TWO *Juliet's bedroom. Lady Capulet and Juliet are discussing Juliet's future marriage plans.*

Lady Capulet Tell me daughter Juliet, how stands your disposition to be married?

Juliet Marriage is an honor that I dream not of.

Lady Capulet Well, think of marriage now; younger than you are made already mothers. Thus then, good news—the valiant Paris seeks you for his love. Tonight you will meet at the masque. What say you? Speak briefly, can you like of Paris' love?

Juliet I'll look to like, if looking liking move.

SCENE THREE *The Capulet masquerade party. The house is beautiful and extravagant. Decorations adorn every corner. Fine food is being served on large trays, and music plays while people dance. Wearing masks, Romeo, Mercutio, and Benvolio hesitate at the door. They look through the window.*

Mercutio Gentle Romeo, you must dance.

Romeo Not I. You have dancing shoes with nimble soles; I have a soul of lead, so stakes me to the ground. I cannot move.

Benvolio Come, knock, and enter; and no sooner in, find a partner and dance.

Romeo I'll just look on.

Mercutio Come, sir, we waste our lights in vain, like lamps by day. Take our good meaning, let us go inside.

Romeo Very well.

The three young men join the party. Romeo immediately notices Juliet, who is dancing. He is completely entranced with her. Romeo approaches a servant of the house.

Romeo What lady's that, dancing with yonder knight?

Servant I know not, sir.

Romeo O! She doth teach the torches to burn bright. Beauty too rich for use, for earth too dear! Did my heart love till now? For I never saw true beauty till this night.

On the balcony above where Romeo is standing, Tybalt watches the scene below. He overhears Romeo asking the servant about Juliet. Tybalt's uncle, Lord Capulet, and his servant, Gregory, are standing nearby.

Tybalt This, by his voice, should be a Montague. *(to Gregory)* Fetch me my sword, boy. Now, by the stock and honor of my kin, to strike him dead, I hold it not a sin.

Lord Capulet How now, Tybalt? Where are you going with that sword?

Tybalt Uncle, a Montague is among us!

Lord Capulet I see, it is young Romeo. Content thee, gentle coz, let him alone. I have heard that he is an honest and noble young man.

Tybalt I won't allow him to stay here! I'll not endure him. *(He begins walking away with his sword.)*

Lord Capulet He will stay! Am I the master here, or you? Go to, you are a saucy boy!

Tybalt I will withdraw, but only for now. This intrusion shall, now seeming sweet, convert to bitter gall.

Exit Tybalt.

Romeo and Juliet begin dancing together. They are holding hands and gazing into each other's eyes. They are falling in love, and neither has felt these emotions before. After the dance, Romeo pulls Juliet aside.

Romeo My lips ready stand to smooth this rough touch with a tender kiss.

Juliet You do wrong your hand too much.

Romeo O dear saint, let lips do what hands do! *(They kiss.)*

Juliet You kiss by the book.

Juliet's nurse interrupts them.

Nurse Madam, your mother wishes a word with you.

Juliet reluctantly pulls away from Romeo, looking back at him over her shoulder as she leaves.

Romeo *(to nurse)* Who is her mother?

Nurse Her mother is the lady of the house.

Romeo Is she a Capulet? Oh dear account! My life is my foe's debt.

Romeo looks upset and walks slowly away.

Romeo Benvolio, Mercutio, let us leave this place.

Lord Capulet Nay, gentlemen, prepare not to be gone. There is more food, and dancing, and music to be heard. You must go? Why then, I thank you all, and good-night.

Re-enter Juliet. She notices Romeo and his friends leaving the party.

Juliet Come hither, nurse. Who is he going out the door?

Nurse His name is Romeo, and a Montague. The only son of your great enemy.

Juliet My only love sprung from my only hate! Too early seen unknown, and known too late! Prodigious birth of love it is to me, that I must love a loathed enemy.

Nurse Come, we must go.

ACT TWO

SCENE ONE *A quiet street outside the Capulet house.*

Benvolio Romeo! Cousin Romeo! He has hid himself among these trees.

Mercutio Romeo, good-night. I'll to my bed. This field is too cold for me to sleep. Come, shall we go?

Benvolio Go, then, for it is in vain to seek him here.

SCENE TWO *Romeo is sitting under a tree near Juliet's balcony, sad from learning Juliet is a Capulet. Suddenly, Juliet appears on her balcony.*

Romeo But, soft! What light through yonder window breaks? It is the east, and Juliet is the sun! It is my lady; it is my love! O, that she knew she were! See how she leans her cheek upon her hand. O, that I were a glove upon that hand, that I might touch that cheek!

Juliet *(thinking she is alone)* Ah me!

Romeo She speaks! O, speak again, bright angel!

Juliet O Romeo, Romeo! Wherefore art thou, Romeo? Deny thy father and refuse thy name. Or, if thou wilt not, be but sworn my love, and I'll no longer be a Capulet.

Romeo Shall I hear more, or shall I speak now?

Juliet It is only thy name that is my enemy. What's in a name? That which we call a rose by any other name would smell as sweet.

Romeo *(to Juliet)* My name is hateful to myself, because it is an enemy to thee.

Juliet Who is there? I have heard fewer than a hundred words from that tongue, yet I know the sound. Art thou not Romeo, and a Montague?

Romeo Neither, fair maid, if either you dislike.

Romeo climbs up onto the balcony.

Juliet They will murder you if they see you here!

Romeo I have night's cloak to hide me from their eyes. And if you dost not love me, then let them find me here. My life were better ended by their hate; than death postponed, living without thy love.

Juliet How did you find this place?

Romeo Love guided me here. I would have gone to the farthest sea to find you.

Juliet You love me? O gentle Romeo! If you love, pronounce it faithfully.

Romeo Lady, by yonder moon I swear.

Juliet Swear not by the inconstant moon.

Romeo What shall I swear by?

Juliet Do not swear at all. I have no joy of this contract tonight. It is too rash, too unadvised, too sudden . . . but if thy bent of love be honorable, thy purpose marriage, send me word tomorrow. And I'll come to thee, and all my fortunes at thy foot I'll lay.

Romeo So thrive my soul!

From within the house, the nurse calls for Juliet.

Juliet *(looking anxiously behind her)* By and by, I come!—When tomorrow shall I send to thee?

Romeo At the hour of nine, my love.

Juliet I will not fail. 'Tis twenty years till then.

Romeo Good-night. Sleep dwell upon thine eyes; peace be with thee.

Romeo begins climbing down from the balcony.

Juliet Good-night, good-night; parting is such sweet sorrow.

SCENE THREE *The next morning in a green, wooded field. Friar Laurence is gathering herbs and berries.*

Enter Romeo from the woods.

Romeo Good morrow, father.

Friar Laurence What early tongue greets me so sweetly? Romeo, you have not been in bed tonight.

Romeo That is true; the sweeter rest was mine. I have been feasting with mine enemy.

Friar Laurence Be plain, good son, and confess what has happened.

Romeo My heart's dear love is set on the fair daughter of rich Capulet. As mine on hers, so hers is set on mine. We met, we woo'd, and made exchange of vow. Pray, consent to marry us today.

Friar Laurence What a change is here! Is Rosaline, whom thou did love so dear, so soon forsaken?

Romeo I pray thee, chide not; she whom I love now doth grace for grace and love for love allow. Rosaline did not so.

Friar Laurence But come young waverer, I will help you. I'll be thy assistant in this. This union may so happy prove, to turn your households' rancor to pure love.

SCENE FOUR *A street near the Montague house. Benvolio and Mercutio are still searching for Romeo.*

Mercutio Where could Romeo be? Came he not home tonight?

Benvolio Not to his father's; I spoke to him. I found out that Tybalt, the kinsman of old Capulet, has sent a letter to his father's house this morning.

Mercutio A challenge to Romeo.

Benvolio Romeo will answer it.

Mercutio That Tybalt is the prince of cats, I tell you. He is the pox of such antic, lisping, affecting fantasticoes!

Enter Romeo.

Benvolio Here comes Romeo.

Romeo Good morrow, friends. What counterfeit did I give you?

Mercutio The slip, sir, the slip.

Romeo Pardon, good Mercutio. My business was great. *(He looks down the street.)* Ah, but who approaches?

Enter Juliet's nurse, approaching the young men.

Nurse Gentlemen, can any of you tell me where I may find young Romeo?

Romeo I am he.

Nurse If you be he, sir, I desire some confidence with you.

Romeo I will follow you.

Benvolio *(joking)* She will likely invite him to supper.

Nurse Sir, a word. My young lady Juliet bade me inquire of your intentions.

Romeo Bid her to meet me at Friar Laurence's cell this afternoon. There, we will be married.

Nurse She will be a joyful woman!

Romeo Commend me to thy lady.

SCENE FIVE *Juliet's bedroom. Juliet has been waiting impatiently for her nurse to return with news from Romeo.*

Juliet The clock struck nine when I sent the nurse. In half an hour she promised to return. Now is the sun upon the highmost hill, and from nine till twelve is three long hours, yet she has not come. But old folks, many feign as they were dead; unwieldy, slow, heavy, and pale as lead.
O, here she comes!

Enter nurse.

Juliet What news, nurse? Hast thou met with him? Please tell me!

Nurse I am weary, give me leave awhile. Fie, how my bones ache! What a jaunt I have had!

Juliet Come, I pray thee, speak, good nurse, speak! What says he of our marriage?

Nurse How my head aches! What a head have I! It beats as it would fall in twenty pieces. And my back, my back!

Juliet I am sorry thou art not well. Sweet nurse, tell me, what says my love?

Nurse Your love is an honest gentleman, and courteous, and kind, and handsome, and—where is your mother?

Juliet Where is my mother? She is in the house. Where should she be? How oddly thou repliest!

Nurse O dear lady! Is this the medicine for my aching bones? Henceforward do your messages yourself.

Juliet Come, what says Romeo?

Nurse Hurry to Friar Laurence's cell. There stays a husband to make you a wife.

Juliet *(hugging the nurse)* Thank you, nurse! Thank you! Farewell!

SCENE SIX *Friar Laurence's cell. Romeo and the friar are waiting anxiously for Juliet.*

Friar Laurence So smile the heavens upon this holy act.

Romeo Do thou but close our hands with holy words, then love-devouring death do what he dare; it is enough I may but call her mine!

Enter Juliet, breathless and excited.

Romeo *(clasping Juliet's hands)* Ah, Juliet! I hope the measure of thy joy is as great as mine!

Juliet If love be riches, my true love has grown to such excess, I cannot sum up half my sum of wealth!

Friar Laurence Come, come with me, and we will make short work. For now, in marriage, we shall join two into one.

Romeo and Juliet kneel as the friar performs the ceremony and pronounces them husband and wife.

⚜ ACT THREE ⚜

SCENE ONE *The marketplace in Verona. It is filled with people vending and buying foods and goods. Mercutio and Benvolio are enjoying the activity of the marketplace when they see several Capulets approaching.*

Benvolio I pray thee, good Mercutio, let's retire. The day is hot, the Capulets abroad, and, if we meet, we shall not escape a brawl. For now, these hot days, is the mad blood stirring.

Mercutio Thy head is as full of quarrels as an egg is full of meat, and yet thou wilt tutor me from quarreling!

Benvolio By my head, here come the Capulets.

Mercutio By my heel, I care not.

Enter Tybalt and several other Capulets.

Tybalt Mercutio, thou consort'st with Romeo . . .

Mercutio Consort! Thou dost make minstrels of us.

Benvolio We talk here in a public place. Let us withdraw to a more private place to air your grievances. Here all eyes gaze upon us.

Mercutio Let them gaze. I will not budge.

Enter Romeo.

Tybalt Well, peace be with you. Here comes my man. Romeo! Thou art a villain.

Romeo Villain I am none. Farewell, for I see thou know'st me not.

Tybalt Boy, this shall not excuse the injuries that thou hast done me. Therefore turn, and draw. *(He draws his sword.)*

Romeo I do protest, I never injured thee. And so, good Capulet—which name I tender as dearly as my own—be satisfied.

Mercutio O dishonorable, vile submission! Tybalt, you rat-catcher, will you walk?

Tybalt What dost thou want with me?

Mercutio King of cats, nothing but one of your nine lives! *(He draws his sword.)*

Tybalt I am for you.

Tybalt and Mercutio begin a furious sword fight.

Romeo Draw, Benvolio! Help me beat down their weapons. Gentlemen, for shame, stop this outrage! Tybalt, Mercutio, the prince has forbidden fighting in Verona streets! Hold, good Mercutio!

Romeo tries to stop the fight by grabbing Mercutio. While Mercutio struggles with Romeo, Tybalt stabs Mercutio.

Mercutio I am hurt! Why came you between us? I was hurt under your arm. Ask for me tomorrow, and you shall find me a grave man.

Romeo I thought all for the best.

Mercutio Help me, Benvolio. A plague on both your houses! They have made worms' meat of me.

Mercutio dies in Romeo's arms.

Romeo Mercutio!

Benvolio O Romeo, brave Mercutio's dead!

Romeo *(to Tybalt)* Either thou, or I, or both, must go with him!

Filled with grief and anger, Romeo picks up Mercutio's sword and begins fighting with Tybalt. Romeo corners him, then stabs him in the heart before he realizes what he has done.

Benvolio Romeo, away! Be gone! The prince will doom thee to death!

Romeo O, I am fortune's fool!

Exit Romeo, running. Enter Prince Escalus, with his officers; Lord and Lady Montague; and Lord and Lady Capulet.

Lady Capulet Tybalt, my cousin! O, the blood is spilled!

Prince Escalus Benvolio, who began this bloody fray?

Benvolio Tybalt, here slain, whom Romeo's hand did slay! Romeo spoke him fair, knees humbly bowed. But Tybalt, deaf to peace, fought with and killed Mercutio. And Romeo, who had but newly entertained revenge, slayed Tybalt before I could stop him.

Lady Capulet I beg for justice. Romeo killed Tybalt; Romeo must not live!

Prince Escalus Romeo slew Tybalt, and he slew Mercutio; who now the price of his dear blood doth owe?

Lord Montague Not Romeo, Prince. Tybalt killed Mercutio, and my son was his friend. His fault concludes but what the law should end—the life of Tybalt.

Prince Escalus For that offense, we do exile Romeo immediately. If he is ever found here again, that hour is his last.

SCENE TWO *Juliet's garden. Juliet is happily picking flowers as her nurse rushes into the garden.*

Nurse He's dead, he's dead! We are undone, lady! Alack the day!

Juliet Has Romeo slain himself? If he be slain, say so; if not, no. Brief sounds determine my weal or woe.

Nurse I saw the wound; I saw it with mine eyes! I nearly fainted at the sight.

Juliet O, break, my heart! Break at once! Vile earth, to earth resign; end motion here!

Nurse O Tybalt, the best friend I had! O courteous Tybalt! That ever I should live to see thee dead! And Romeo, who killed him, banished!

Juliet O no! Did Romeo's hand shed Tybalt's blood?

Nurse It did, it did; alas the day, it did!

Juliet O serpent heart, hid with a flowering face! O, that deceit should dwell in such a gorgeous place!

Nurse There's no trust, no faith, no honesty in men! These griefs, these woes, these sorrows make me old. Shame come to Romeo!

Juliet Blistered be thy tongue for such a wish!

Nurse Will you speak well of him that killed your cousin?

Juliet Shall I speak ill of him that is my husband? That villain Tybalt would have killed him. But now he is banished—there is no measure in that word's death!

Nurse Hurry to your chamber. I'll find Romeo to comfort you. He will be here tonight. He's hid in Friar Laurence's cell.

Juliet O, go to him! Give this ring to my true knight, and bid him come to take his last farewell.

SCENE THREE *Friar Laurence's cell. Romeo waits for news of Prince Escalus' decision about his fate.*

Enter Friar Lawrence.

Friar Laurence Romeo, come forth; come forth, fearful man. Thou art wedded to calamity.

Romeo Friar, what news? Am I to die?

Friar Laurence Not death, but banishment from Verona henceforth.

Romeo I may as well be dead. There is no world without Verona walls.

Friar Laurence Be patient, for the world is broad and wide. This is dear mercy, though you see it not.

Romeo It is torture, not mercy! Heaven is here, where Juliet lives. Every cat, dog, and little mouse may look upon my Juliet. Yet I cannot. This is mercy?

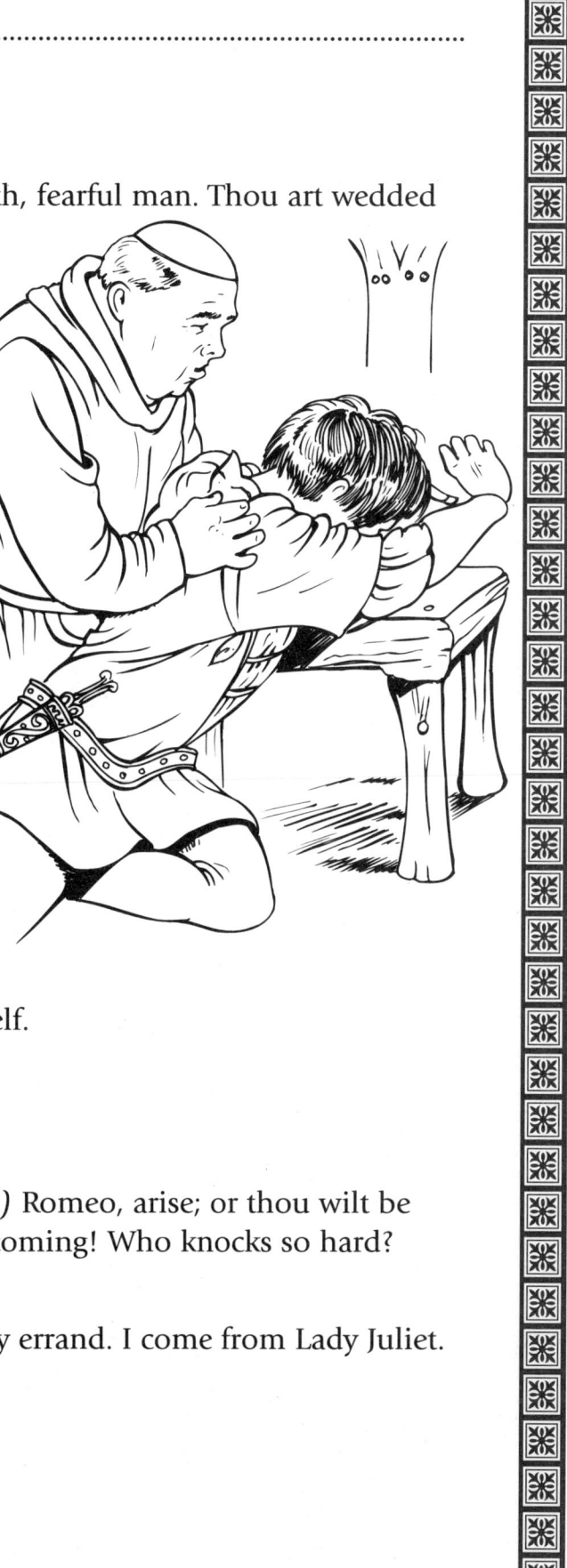

There is knocking at the door.

Friar Laurence Arise, good Romeo; hide thyself.

Knocking is heard again, louder this time.

Friar Laurence Hark, who's there? *(whispering)* Romeo, arise; or thou wilt be taken. Run to my study. *(shouting loudly)* I am coming! Who knocks so hard? What's your will?

Nurse Let me come in, and you shall know my errand. I come from Lady Juliet.

Friar Laurence Welcome then.

Enter nurse.

Romeo Nurse!

Nurse Ah sir! Well, death's the end of all.

Romeo Speak'st thou of Juliet? How is it with her? Does she not think of me an old murderer? What says she to our cancelled love?

Nurse She says nothing, sir, but weeps and weeps, falling down on her bed, crying your name and Tybalt's.

Romeo As if my name, shot from the deadly level of a gun, did murder her. O, tell me, friar, in what vile part of this anatomy does my name lodge? Tell me, so I can remove the hateful part with my sword! *(He draws his sword.)*

Friar Laurence Hold thy desperate hand. Art thou a man? Thy tears are womanish. Nurse, tell thy lady, Juliet, that Romeo is coming.

Nurse Yes, my lord. *(She hands Romeo the ring.)* I'll tell my lady you will come. Here, sir, a ring she bid me to give you. Make haste, for it grows very late.

Exit nurse.

Romeo How well my comfort is revived by this!

Friar Laurence Go hence. But be gone by the break of day and sojourn to Mantua. There you shall live until we can find a time to blaze your marriage, reconcile your friends, beg pardon of the prince, and call thee back, with twenty hundred thousand times more joy than when thou went forth in sorrow.

Romeo But that a joy past joy calls out on me. Farewell, friar!

SCENE FOUR *The Capulet house. Lord and Lady Capulet and Paris are discussing Paris' upcoming marriage to Juliet.*

Paris These times of woe afford no time to woo. Madam, good-night; commend me to your daughter.

Lady Capulet I will, and know her mind early tomorrow.

Lord Capulet Wife, acquaint her here of Paris' love; and bid her that on Thursday, she shall be married to this noble earl. *(to Paris)* Will you be ready? Do you like this haste? What say you to Thursday?

Paris My lord, I would that Thursday were tomorrow.

Lady Capulet I'll tell Juliet. Good-night.

SCENE FIVE *Juliet's chamber. Romeo and Juliet are holding each other and discussing their future.*

Romeo Night's candles are burnt out, and the day stands tiptoe on the misty mountain tops. I must be gone and live, or stay and die.

Juliet The light is not daylight, I know it. It is some meteor cast from the sun to light thy way to the city of Mantua. Therefore stay, thou need not be gone yet.

Enter nurse.

Nurse Madam! Your lady mother is coming to your chamber. The day is broke. Be wary, look about!

Juliet Then, window, let day in, and let life out.

Romeo Farewell, farewell! One kiss, and I'll descend.

They kiss, and Romeo begins climbing down the balcony.

Juliet Art thou gone so? My love, husband, friend! In every minute there will be many days. By this count I shall be much in years before again I behold my Romeo.

Romeo Farewell!

Juliet Do you think we shall ever meet again?

Romeo I doubt it not. And all these woes shall serve for sweet discourse in our time to come. Adieu!

Exit Romeo.

Lady Capulet *(from outside the bedroom)* Daughter, are you awake?

Juliet Who is it that calls? It is my lady mother. What brings her so early?

Juliet lies down on her bed. Enter Lady Capulet, who sits down beside her.

Lady Capulet Why, how now, Juliet?

Juliet Madam, I am not well.

Lady Capulet Still weeping for your Tybalt? You had much love for your cousin.

Juliet Let me weep for such loss.

Lady Capulet Thou should weep not so much for his death, but that the villain lives who slaughtered him. That villain Romeo. We will have vengeance for it, fear thou not.

Juliet Indeed, I shall never be satisfied.

Lady Capulet But now I'll tell thee joyful tidings, girl.

Juliet Joy comes well in such a needy time. What are they, I beseech your ladyship?

Lady Capulet Thou hast a loving father, child, who has sorted out a sudden day of joy, one that you expected not.

Juliet Madam, in happy time, what day is that?

Lady Capulet Marry the gallant young and noble gentleman Paris next Thursday morn.

Juliet Tell my father that I will *not* marry yet; and when I do, it shall be Romeo whom you know I hate, rather than Paris!

Lady Capulet *(surprised and angry)* Here comes your father; tell him so yourself.

Enter Lord Capulet.

Lord Capulet How now, wife? Have you delivered to her our decree?

Lady Capulet Ay, sir; but she will have none of it.

Lord Capulet She is too proud! Does she not count herself blessed to marry so worthy a gentleman?

Juliet Good father, I beg you on my knees. Hear me with patience but to speak a word!

Lord Capulet If you do not marry Paris on this Thursday, I'll never acknowledge thee again! Nor what is mine shall never do thee good!

Exit Lord Capulet and his wife.

Juliet O nurse! How shall this be prevented?

Nurse I think it best you marry Paris. He is a lovely gentleman, and your first husband may as well be dead as banished. Living here, you have no use of him.

Juliet *(shocked)* Speak'st thou from thy heart?

Nurse And from my soul too.

Juliet Well, thou hast comforted me. Go in and tell my mother I am going to Friar Laurence's cell to make confession.

Exit nurse.

Juliet O most wicked fiend! I'll to the friar, to know his remedy. If all else fail, myself have the power to die.

⚜ ACT FOUR ⚜

SCENE ONE *Friar Laurence's cell. Paris is visiting Friar Laurence to make wedding arrangements for he and Juliet.*

Friar Laurence On Thursday, sir? The time is very short.

Paris My father Capulet will have it so; and I am nothing slow, to slack his haste.

Enter Juliet.

Paris Happily met, my lady and my wife!

Juliet That may be, sir, when I may be a wife.

Paris That may be, must be, love, on Thursday next.

Friar Laurence My lord, Paris, we must entreat the time alone.

Paris Very well. Juliet, I will awaken thee early Thursday. Till then, adieu.

Exit Paris.

Juliet O, shut the door! Father, come weep with me; I am past hope, past cure, past help!

Friar Laurence I have a plan, if you dare.

Juliet I shall, if I am reunited with my Romeo.

Friar Laurence Go home then, and agree to marry Paris. Tomorrow night is the night before your wedding. When you are alone, take thou this vial and drink from it. *(He hands Juliet a vial of liquid.)* You will seem dead for forty-two hours, then you will awaken as from a pleasant sleep. In the meantime, I shall send a letter to Romeo. He shall come and watch thy waking. And that very night shall Romeo bear thee to Mantua with him.

Juliet *(taking the vial)* Give it to me!

Friar Laurence Be strong and prosperous in this resolve. I'll send a friar with speed to Mantua with my letters to Romeo.

Juliet Love give me strength! Farewell, dear father.

SCENE TWO *A room in the Capulet house.*

Lord Capulet How now, my headstrong daughter! Where have you been?

Juliet Where I have learned to repent the sin of disobedience. I beg your pardon, Father, for disobeying your wishes. I shall marry Paris.

Lord Capulet This is as it should be. My heart is wondrous light, now that my girl has come to her senses!

SCENE THREE *The night before Juliet's and Paris' wedding. Juliet and her nurse are discussing the wedding in Juliet's chamber.*

Juliet Those clothes will be fine. But nurse, I pray thee, leave me to myself tonight.

Enter Lady Capulet.

Lady Capulet What, are you busy? Need you my help?

Juliet No, madam; we have everything prepared for tomorrow. So please, let me now be left alone.

Lady Capulet Good-night. Get some rest; you will need it.

Exit Lady Capulet and nurse.

Juliet *(whispering)* Farewell! I hope we shall meet again. Come, vial. *(She picks up the vial and drinks from it.)* Romeo, I come! This I drink to thee! *(She falls asleep.)*

SCENE FOUR *Juliet's Chamber the next morning. It is Juliet's and Paris' wedding day.*

Enter nurse. She has come to awaken Juliet.

Nurse Lady Juliet, wake up. *(She shakes Juliet gently.)* Why, lamb! Why, lady! What! Not a word? *(She shakes Juliet again, and then realizes she is dead.)* Help! O lamentable day! Juliet! Juliet!

Enter Lady Capulet.

Lady Capulet What is the matter? *(She notices Juliet's lifeless body.)* O me, O me! My child, my only life! She's dead! She's dead!

⚜ ACT FIVE ⚜

SCENE ONE *A lonely street in Mantua. Romeo is waiting for word about Juliet from his servant Balthasar.*

Enter Balthasar.

Romeo What news from Verona? How is my lady? How is my Juliet?

Balthasar I have just seen Juliet laid to rest in the Capulet vault. O, pardon me for bringing these ill news.

Romeo Juliet, dead? Thou art deceived! Have you no letters from the friar?

Balthasar No, my good lord.

Romeo *(devastated)* No matter; get thee gone.

Exit Balthasar.

Romeo Well, Juliet, I will lie with thee tonight.—What, ho! Apothecary!

Enter apothecary.

Romeo Let me have a dram of poison that will disperse itself through all the veins, that the life-weary taker may fall dead.

Apothecary Such mortal drugs I have, but I cannot sell them under Mantua law.

Romeo You are very poor, and I have much money to give you.

Apothecary My poverty, but not my will, consents.

The apothecary takes the coins and hands Romeo the poison.

SCENE TWO *Friar Laurence's cell. Friar Laurence waits for Friar John to return from Mantua.*

Enter Friar John.

Friar Laurence Welcome from Mantua. What says Romeo?

Friar John I could not deliver your letter to Romeo. I had stopped to visit a sick friend, and one of our order sealed up the doors to keep the infectious disease from spreading.

Friar Laurence Unhappy fortune! The letter was of dear import! The neglecting of it may do much danger. Now I must to the monument alone. I will fetch Juliet and keep her at my cell until Romeo comes!

SCENE THREE *The Capulet vault. Many pedastools holding the Capulet dead rest inside the dark tunnels. Juliet rests next to Tybalt's body. Paris kneels next to her.*

Paris Sweet flower, with flowers thy bridal bed I strew. O lovely Juliet! *(He hears footsteps approaching the vault, and he crouches behind Juliet's pedastool.)*

Enter Romeo.

Paris The banished Montague that murdered my love's cousin! *(He stands.)* Condemned villain! I will apprehend thee! Thou must die!

Romeo Good gentle youth, tempt not a desperate man.

Paris I do defy you! I will apprehend thee for a felon here!

Romeo Wilt thou provoke me? Then, have at thee, boy!

They draw their swords and fight. Romeo stabs and kills Paris. Sadly, he places Paris' body next to Tybalt's. He sits next to Juliet.

Romeo O my love! My wife! Death, that has sucked the honey of thy breath has had no power yet upon thy beauty. Eyes, look your last! Arms, take your last embrace! *(He hugs her.)* Here's to my love! *(He drinks the poison.)* O apothecary! Thy drugs are quick. Thus with a kiss, I die. *(He kisses Juliet, and falls dead.)*

Enter Friar Laurence. He sees the bodies of Romeo and Paris.

Friar Laurence What blood is this? Romeo! And Paris, too? What an unkind hour is guilty of this lamentable chance!

Juliet begins to wake up.

Friar Laurence The lady stirs.

Juliet Friar, where is my Romeo?

Friar Laurence Come, good Juliet. Thy husband lies dead. And Paris, too. *(They hear footsteps approaching from outside the tomb.)* I hear some noise. Let me take you from this place.

The footsteps get louder.

Friar Laurence I dare no longer stay! Come, Juliet! *(He leaves, thinking Juliet is following behind him.)*

Juliet Go, get thee hence, for I will not away. *(She kneels next to Romeo's body.)* What's this? A vial? Poison, I see, has been his timeless end. *(She tries to drink from the vial.)* Churl! Drunk all, and left no friendly drop for me? I shall kiss thy lips, then. Hopefully, some poison yet hangs on them. *(She kisses him, finding no poison there either.)* Thy lips are warm.

The footsteps are louder. Juliet now hears voices as well.

Juliet Yea, noise? Then I'll be brief. *(She takes Romeo's dagger.)* O happy dagger! This is thy sheath! *(She stabs herself and falls over on Romeo, dead.)*

Enter Prince Escalus, his officers, Lord Montague, and Lord and Lady Capulet.

Lord Montague Alas, my liege. My wife is dead tonight after hearing of my son's exile. What else can happen to make it worse?

Prince Escalus Look, and thou shall see.

Lord Montague and the Capulets turn to see their only children lying dead. Re-enter Friar Laurence.

Lord Capulet O wife! Look how our daughter bleeds!

Prince Escalus Quiet your outrage until we can find out what happened here.

Friar Laurence I will be brief. Romeo, there dead, was husband to that Juliet. I married them; and their stolen marriage-day was Tybalt's doomsday. When Juliet became betrothed to Paris, she came to me to rid her from this second marriage. I gave her a sleeping potion which wrought on her the form of death. I wrote to Romeo that he should come here tonight. But Friar John was stayed in Verona by accident, and could not deliver the letter. When I came here tonight to fetch Juliet to my cell, here lay the noble Paris and true Romeo, dead. She awoke; and I entreated her to come forth, but she did violence on herself.

Prince Escalus Capulet! Montague! See, what a scourge is laid upon your hate, that heaven finds means to kill your joys with love.

Lord Capulet *(holding out his hand)* O brother Montague, give me thy hand.

Lord Montague *(taking Lord Capulet's hand)* I can give thee more; a statue of gold will be raised of Juliet.

Prince Escalus A glooming peace this morning with it brings. The sun for sorrow will not show his head. Go hence, and talk more of these sad things. Some shall be pardoned, and some punished. For never was there a story of more woe, than this of Juliet and her Romeo.

VOCABULARY

PROLOGUE

ancient very old; in existence for many years

civil of or belonging to citizens

dignity worth; esteem

fair beautiful

fatal destined for ruin or death

grudge deep resentment; unwilling to forgive

households families

misadventured unfortunate

mutiny conflict

piteous full of pity

strife conflict

ACT ONE

coz cousin or other relative

dejected depressed

disposition mood

extravagant excessively fancy; elaborate

gall injury; hurt

hither here

kin family; relation

loathed hated

look to like hope to like

masque masquerade party

mistempered made for evil purpose

my life is my foe's debt my happiness is in my enemy's hands

nimble quick

prodigious feeling that evil may come; ominous

rank offensive; corrupt

rebellious to act out against authority

saucy overbearing; insulting

subjects people of the city

sups eats; dines

thither forward

valiant brave; noble

wither to where

yonder over there

you kiss by the book you kiss as if you had studied it and know the rules well

ACT TWO

affecting imitating

antic grotesque

bade commanded

bent intensity; endurance

breaks comes forth; reveals

chide scold

commend deliver

counterfeit deceit; falsity

devouring using up; destroying

fantasticoes absurd, irrational people

feign pretend

fie expression of disgust

forsaken given up; forgotten

henceforward from now on

inconstant changes frequently without reason

jaunt short trip

lisping speaking childishly

pox curse

rancor ill will; bad feelings

stays waits

thrive grow; flourish

unwieldy awkward; cumbersome

vain useless

wherefore why

woo'd exchanged affections

VOCABULARY

ACT THREE

acquaint make familiar

adieu good-bye

alack expression of sorrow or regret

banished forced to leave one's home or city; exiled

beseech beg; plead

bid command

blaze to make public

brawl fight

cat object of disgust or aversion

chamber bedroom

consort'st share company; make music with

decree decision; command

discourse talk; conversation

draw take out a weapon and prepare to fight

entertained thought about

exile forced to leave one's home or city; banishment

fray fight; argument

henceforth in the future

humbly without pride or arrogance

minstrels musicians

reconcile restore friendship

resign give up; submit

revived brought back to life

slay kill

sojourn temporary stay

submission to give in

tender regard; care for

vile disgusting

walk step away from everyone

wary careful of surroundings

weal general welfare; well-being

wedded to calamity married to misery

woe grief; lament

ACT FOUR

bear carry; bring forth

entreat enter in conversation

haste speed

headstrong not easily given to advice or suggestions

lamentable sorrowful; sad

prosperous successful

resolve firm decision; purpose

slack neglectful of

vial small bottle

ACT FIVE

apothecary seller of medicine

apprehend arrest; seize

betrothed engaged; promised

churl rude fellow

dagger knife

devastated overwhelmed with grief

disperse distribute

dram small amount

felon evil, wicked criminal

get thee hence go away from here

import importance

infectious contagious; easily spread

liege one's superior

mortal deadly

poverty lack of money; state of being poor

provoke urge to take action

scourge punishment

sheath case for a knife's blade

strew spread out

wrought brought on

INTRODUCING DRAMA

 "All the world's a stage, and all the men and women merely players." This quote from Shakespeare's delightful comedy *As You Like It* is a great way to begin your study of Shakespeare. Ask students what they think this quote means. Explain that "players" are actually "actors." Shakespeare meant that throughout our lives, we play many different roles—children, teenagers, and adults; daughters, sons, mothers, fathers, cousins, friends, workers, and so on. We also "act" within our life roles. Play-acting is a part of everyday existence. Ask students when they might "act" in real life. Invite them to act out an incident from their lives for the class (for example, a problem with a sibling, a funny incident with a family member or friend, or an embarrassing moment). Students can have lots of fun with this; encourage them to be creative, yet true to life.

 Ask students if they have ever seen a stage play. Discuss the difference between acting onstage, in the movies, or on TV. In Shakespeare's time, there were no TVs, movies, radios, or video games, so entertainment usually came in the form of drama. Drama did not begin with Shakespeare. Plays were watched with rapt attention by theatregoers many centuries before him. Drama is thought to have developed from many sources—an outgrowth of religious ceremonies to appease the gods; songs at grave sites or about heroes, extolling their virtues; to preach morals to the masses; and simply to satisfy people's natural love for storytelling and entertainment. Drama was and still is a way to "get away from it all" and have a good time. It creates an opportunity for us to laugh at ourselves as we see life reflected in the many human characters and situations portrayed before us.

 Showing videotapes of Shakespearean plays helps children understand the nuances of drama, and how Shakespeare's language and characterization bring his stories to life. Many of Shakespeare's plays are available on videotape. Watch a video and/or compare one video interpretation to another. For example, Franco Zeffirelli's 1968 film version of *Romeo and Juliet* is a classically authentic and well-done adaptation. There are several adaptations to use for comparison, including the "modernized" 1996 version, and even *West Side Story*, a movie that places the doomed lovers in the midst of a 1950s Brooklyn gang feud. Make sure to view videos before showing them to your class, as some material may be unsuitable due to language or adult situations. However, don't let videos replace the reading and performing of plays by your students. Shakespeare is meant to be experienced as a live performance.

ELEMENTS OF A STORY

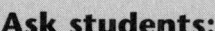

Before reading the summary of the play to your students, familiarize them with the elements of a story. Write the following terms on the board and discuss what they mean with students. Tell them to look for these story elements and consider these questions as they listen to the play's summary.

Protagonist—hero

Antagonist—villain

Sequence—the order in which events occur

Suspense—the tension and excitement created by not knowing a story's outcome

Plot—what the story is about

Climax—the scene or event with the highest dramatic tension (suspense) that creates the most drama or brings about a turning point in the action

Dialogue—words spoken by the characters

Ask students:

- **Who do you think is the protagonist? the antagonist? Does a story need both a protagonist and antagonist? Why?** (*to provide conflict, interest, and contrast*)

- **Did events in the story happen sequentially? Was there an easily-identifiable beginning, middle, and end? Why is sequence important in a story?** (*so readers won't be confused; so the story makes sense*)

- **Was the plot believable? Did it keep you interested?**

- **Was the story suspenseful? Were you anxious about what was going to happen? What part or parts of the story were most suspenseful?**

- **What scene or scenes were the climax of the story? Was there a particular event that sealed the fate of the protagonists?**

- **Did the language and dialogue seem authentic and the emotions true to life?**

THE LANGUAGE OF SHAKESPEARE

At first, "Shakespearean language" can seem overwhelming to students. Many students have heard Shakespeare quoted, but have no idea what these quotes means. Though the language may seem complex, it was common in England at the time the plays were written. It's no wonder students may feel overwhelmed reading even an edited version of a Shakespearean play. It's been estimated that he uses between 25,000 and 29,000 different words in his plays and poems! But among all the "thees" and "thous" are many common, everyday expressions students will be amazed to know originated with Shakespeare (or "the bard"). Write several of these Shakespearean expressions on the board and invite students to guess what they mean. They'll be surprised at how these expressions have endured through time.

- Apple of her eye
- Bated breath
- Budge an inch
- Dead as a door nail
- Eating me out of house and home
- Eyesore
- For goodness' sake
- The game is up
- Good riddance
- Green-eyed monster
- Household words
- Knock, knock, who's there?
- Laughingstock
- The naked truth
- Neither rhyme nor reason
- One fell swoop
- The primrose path
- Such stuff as dreams are made on
- Suit the action to the word
- Sweets to the sweet
- To thine own self be true
- Too much of a good thing
- Tower of strength
- Wear my heart on my sleeve
- What's done is done

© 1997 Good Apple

Romeo and Juliet 47

LET'S PUT ON A PLAY!

If you decide to produce the play, you can make it as small or as large a production as you like. You may decide on just an "in-class" production, maybe inviting one or two classes to the performance; or you may want to perform for parents or the whole school. Decide which experience would most benefit your students and meet your classroom needs. When deciding the kind of production you want, consider the time you will need to invest and your classroom budget. It's advantageous for students to be able to perform more than once so they can evaluate and discuss areas for improvement.

Discuss with students which type of production they prefer. Do they want a "classic" Shakespearean production, or do they want to get creative with their interpretation? Students can modernize the play, set it in a different time and/or place, or they can interject their own vernacular. There are many innovative ways to approach a Shakespearean production, so encourage students to brainstorm how they can make theirs original and interesting. Remind them that the fun of putting on a play is in the *process*, not necessarily the *performance*. Make it simple (props, costumes, scenery) so students will get the most out of the experience.

When deciding the kind of production you want, consider the time you will need to invest and your classroom budget.

Most students will want to act in the play, and there's a good chance that several will want the leading roles of Romeo and Juliet. Since one purpose of performing plays is to increase self-esteem and self-confidence, it wouldn't make sense to choose only the most poised, confident students in the class. On the other hand, choosing a cast of shy, introverted actors will lessen the strength of and interest in the play. If possible, try and balance your cast. It's also helpful to choose actors who will help each other develop their parts in the friendly spirit of cooperation. Since there are fewer female than male roles, allow girls to play boys' parts and vice versa. Consider the following questions when choosing actors.

- Does the student have a voice that carries? If not, can he or she bring up the voice level?

- Does the student show imagination and enthusiasm for the part?

- Does he or she have "stage presence"?

- Can the student think on his or her feet and bring the role to life?

LET'S PUT ON A PLAY!

 Auditions can be intimidating and possibly embarrassing for many students. Instead of having them audition for the entire class, invite small student groups to audition different roles for the play. During tryouts, encourage students to offer encouragement and constructive criticism. "Can you look more at the audience?" is obviously better than "He never looks at the audience. He's terrible!" Before tryouts begin, discuss with students how to give constructive criticism in a kind, helpful, and respectful way. Write a list of rules on the board (e.g., *Be positive; Critique the "work," not the person;* and so on). As an alternative, invite students to write comments on note cards and give them to you. Read only those comments that are truly "constructive" and helpful to the performing student. Remind students that there is no one "right" way to do Shakespeare. A diversity of characterizations only adds dimension to the production. Invite groups to brainstorm each role and discuss their ideas with auditioning students.

Critique the "work," not the person.

 Even if your class is large, you can still get everyone involved in the production. Many students will want to act in the play, but some may prefer to work "behind the scenes." Emphasize that *all* jobs are important to a production. Invite interested students to "apply" for the following jobs by writing a short paragraph about why they would be good at a particular task, or you can simply hold "interviews" with individual students. Encourage them to have first and second choices, so everyone has a chance to do something he or she enjoys.

DIRECTOR
You may want to assume this responsibility, using one or two student assistants. The director helps place actors and scenery in the correct places, reminds actors when and how to project their voices, and keeps rehearsals structured. This is a difficult task, so make sure you choose students who aren't too "bossy." Many a production has crumbled because everyone resented the director's bossy ways.

UNDERSTUDIES
Necessary only for the leading roles. If there is more than one performance, they may play the leads the second time.

PROMPTER
Stands offstage during rehearsals and performances, and whispers lines and/or hints for the actors in case they forget their lines or where they should be onstage.

STAGE MANAGER AND ASSISTANT
Ensure that production is going smoothly and all scenery and props are in place.

MAKEUP ARTISTS
Decide on and apply makeup to actors before performances. You may want to have two or three students for this job. Call local cosmetology schools or colleges with theater departments for help.

© 1997 Good Apple   Romeo and Juliet 49

LET'S PUT ON A PLAY!

COSTUMERS
Research the time period in which the play takes place, and create costumes from available materials. (Ask parents to donate old clothes and fabric scraps.) Simple costumes such as tunics can be made from large shirts cinched with belts, and sweatpants can be pulled up to look like Renaissance-period pants.

LIGHTING SPECIALIST
Works with the director to manipulate lighting for dramatic effects.

CURTAIN SPECIALIST
Raises and lowers the curtain at the appropriate times.

SCENERY AND PROP CREW
Finds and/or makes appropriate scenery and props for the play, sets up and takes down scenery during performances, and cleans the stage and "theater" after performances.

ADVERTISING AND PUBLICITY CREW
Makes posters advertising the play. If you're inviting the whole school, write ads about the play and have them announced over the school intercom. If your production is going to be large, you might consider advertising it in your local newspaper or on your local public-access channel.

PLAYBILL WRITERS AND ILLUSTRATORS
Design and write a simple playbill with short blurbs about Shakespeare, the play, actors, scenes, and so on. This will add a nice dimension to your production.

TICKET TAKER
Necessary if you have parents coming to the performances. Most school plays are free, but you can "sell" tickets in exchange for a can of food for a local homeless shelter, a can of pet food or supplies for a local animal shelter, or other charitable donations.

USHERS
Show people to their seats and make certain "unruly" students keep quiet during performances.

VIDEOGRAPHER
Videotapes performances. This is great not only for critiquing the play later, but also authenticates the experience for students. They will love watching themselves on television. You may even want to make copies for families and friends to keep!

Romeo and Juliet
performed by
Room 10

Two star-crossed lovers defy their feuding families to hold onto their love.

JOURNAL/DISCUSSION TOPICS

To inspire students to think critically and form opinions, offer several of the following journal ideas for discussion, reflection, and writing.

ACT ONE

▨ Lord and Lady Capulet are concerned that their daughter hasn't yet married. They choose Paris because he is a noble, wealthy gentleman. If your parents chose a mate for you, what qualities would they look for? How would their choice differ from yours? Explain.

▨ The names *Benvolio* and *Mercutio* actually mean *benevolent (kindhearted)* and *impulsive*. How do the meanings of their names reflect their personalities? Do you think Shakespeare gave them these names on purpose? Why? Write about the history behind your name. Who named you? What does your name mean? If you could choose a different name, what would it be and why?

▨ When Romeo first sees Juliet, he asks himself, "Did my heart love till now?" Just moments earlier he had claimed to love Rosaline. What is the difference between love and infatuation?

▨ Define romantic love. How is it different from love of family? friends? pets? What do you think is the perfect age to fall in love? Why?

▨ In the beginning of the play, Verona witnesses a huge brawl between the Montagues and Capulets. Knowing how violence upsets the citizens of Verona, Prince Escalus claims that anyone seen fighting within the city walls will be put to death. Violence often has a lasting effect on those who witness it. Describe the most violent incident you have ever seen. How did it affect you, and how were you able to deal with the aftermath?

ACT TWO

▨ Romeo's best friend Mercutio is lively, funny, and witty, while Romeo is melancholy and thoughtful. Write about a friend who is different than you, but who you like because of those differences. Why is it fun to be around this person?

© 1997 Good Apple

JOURNAL/DISCUSSION TOPICS

※ In the balcony scene, Juliet claims that her and Romeo's love is "too rash, too unadvised, too sudden." What does she mean by this? Is love more stable when it takes time and effort to develop? What happens when love moves too quickly? Do you agree with Juliet?

※ Friar Laurence advises both Romeo and Juliet in this story. Everyone needs someone to talk to at one time or another. Is there someone in your life who you can always go to for help? Who is this person and how does he or she help you? Tell about a time you sought advice from this person. Did you follow the advice? What happened?

※ Romeo and Juliet marry without their parents' knowledge. Do you think this is a good idea? How would your family be affected if you or one of your siblings did this? Do you think keeping secrets like this lead to positive results? negative results? Why?

※ Rather than seeking out Romeo for revenge at the Capulets' party, Tybalt writes Romeo a letter challenging him to a duel. What do you think of this old-fashioned type of revenge? What are its advantages? disadvantages? How is it different from how revenge is dealt with today?

∞ ACT THREE ∞

※ Mercutio is so upset by Tybalt's insults to Romeo that Mercutio gives his life to defend his friend's good name. Is it right to fight someone else's battles? Often people prefer not to get involved. Are there times when it's good to get involved in someone else's battle? Explain.

※ Prejudice is a central theme in *Romeo and Juliet*. The Montagues and Capulets are prejudiced against each other because a feud has existed for many years. They know nothing about each other personally, yet they hate each other. Many people in the play are hurt by this prejudice. Where do we see prejudice today and what results from it?

※ Romeo and Juliet have only one night together before tragedy befalls them. If you only had one day to spend with a family member or friend, and money was no consideration, what would you do?

JOURNAL/DISCUSSION TOPICS

✺ Lord Capulet threatens to throw Juliet out of the house and never speak to her again if she refuses to marry Paris. This may seem too harsh a punishment. Describe the time when you were in the most trouble with your parents. What was the problem? the punishment?

✺ Romeo is devastated when Prince Escalus banishes him from Verona. Imagine what it would be like to be banished from your home town or city. Describe how you would feel and how you would deal with this situation.

∞ ACT FOUR ∞

✺ Juliet must follow her father's wishes and marry Paris or be thrown out of the house and disowned. What does this and other examples in the story tell us about the status of women during this time in history? If this story took place today, how might it be different?

✺ In the past, many cultures believed in arranged marriages. Romeo and Juliet want to marry for love, an uncommon practice at that time. Can you think of some advantages to arranged marriages? What are some pros and cons of both arranged marriages and marrying for love?

✺ Juliet feels her nurse has betrayed her by encouraging her to forget about Romeo and marry Paris. Describe a time when you felt betrayed or let down by someone. What happened, and how did you resolve it?

✺ Lord and Lady Capulet, the nurse, and Paris are all overcome with sadness at Juliet's apparent death. Write a eulogy for Juliet from the perspective of one of these characters. What thoughts might be going through his or her mind? Might there be some regrets as to how he or she treated Juliet?

✺ Juliet takes a big risk by drinking the "potion" Friar Laurence gives her. She could possibly never wake up again, Romeo may not find her, or she could wake up in the family tomb alone among her dead relatives. Do you think love is worth this kind of sacrifice? What other options could Juliet have considered, or do you think she had no choice? What would you be willing to risk for your one true love?

JOURNAL/DISCUSSION TOPICS

ACT FIVE

▨ Deception plays a major role in the story's outcome. Who deceives who in the story? Perhaps if one person had told the truth, he or she could have changed the story's tragic end. Choose a character in the play who lied, and explain how the story might be different if he or she had told the truth (e.g., Romeo, Juliet, the nurse, or Friar Laurence).

▨ The play would not have developed as it did if not for the ideals and customs of Verona in the 1500s. How does the time and place of the story influence its outcome?

▨ Some people say that revenge destroys both avenger and victim. Would you say this is true for the play? What are some examples of when revenge led to tragedy? How might one of the story's characters have handled his or her situation in a less violent or aggressive way?

▨ In Shakespearean tragedies, a character contributes to his or her own sad ending because of a "fatal flaw." Do you think Romeo and Juliet have flaws that determine their sad end? If so, what are they? Write one or two sentences that describe what makes this play a tragedy.

▨ Imagine for a moment that Juliet woke up right before Romeo drank the poison. What might have happened if their parents found them in the tomb together alive? Do you think they would accept their children's marriage? Explain whether you think the feud would have ended like Friar Laurence hoped, and give reasons supporting your answer.

EXTENSION ACTIVITIES

PROLOGUE PROPS

The prologue to *Romeo and Juliet* tells the audience what will happen in the play. Since language in this passage will seem complicated to students, use this activity to help clarify its meaning. Divide the class into groups of four or five. Give each group a copy of the prologue, a dictionary, old magazines, and access to classroom objects. Invite groups to study the prologue and decide how they will present it to the class using items in the classroom as props. While one student reads aloud, others in the group can hold up props, drawn pictures, magazine cutouts, and so on. (For example, a plastic knife for *fatal*, a picture of a movie star with a cross drawn over his or her head for *star-crossed*, and so on.) This encourages students to pay close attention to every word in the prologue, look up words they don't know (there will be many), and think about the intended messages and themes. After each group has given a presentation, discuss the prologue as a class.

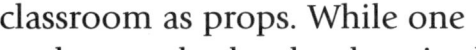

ALAKAZAM! YOU'RE SHAKESPEARE

Invite students to write "Shakespeare style." Divide the class into groups of four or five, and have each group choose a short passage from a favorite story or play. Have students rewrite the chosen passage imitating Shakespeare's beautiful prose and verse. Provide each group with a list of common words found in Shakespeare's work for reference. (Include words such as *doth, hither, thee, wilt, fair, bid, adieu,* and so on.) Have volunteers type the passages into a computer, using special fonts and designs. Invite students to illustrate the designed pages, and then bind them into a class book. As an extension, invite students to rewrite a passage from the play in their own chosen "language" (e.g., as a rapper, alien, surfer, and so on).

© 1997 Good Apple

EXTENSION ACTIVITIES

IMPROMPTU PERFORMANCES

After reading and discussing the summary of the play, divide the class into seven or eight groups and distribute a summary to each. Have groups decide where they think the summary should be broken down into scenes. Depending on your class size, have groups each take responsibility for performing one or two scenes for the class. Invite groups to perform using their own interpretation and language. Students will enjoy using their own "lingo," and you will be amazed to see the play come to life with students' own words and emotions.

Before groups perform, have them write a short summary of the scenes for which they are responsible. For example:

Scene 1—The Capulets and Montagues get into a fight in the town square. The prince comes and tells them that if anyone fights in Verona again, he or she will be put to death.

Scene 2—Romeo and Benvolio find out from Sampson, the Capulets' servant, that there is a masquerade party at the Capulets' that evening. Romeo and Benvolio decide to go in disguise.

Scene 3—Lady Capulet, Juliet, and her nurse talk in Juliet's bedroom. Lady Capulet tells her daughter she is concerned that Juliet hasn't married yet. She invites her to meet Paris at that evening's party.

Scene 4—At the masque, Romeo notices Juliet right away and asks her to dance. They immediately fall in love. Tybalt notices Romeo and wants to challenge him to a fight, but Lord Capulet won't let Tybalt disturb the party.

Scene 5—Benvolio and Mercutio search for Romeo after the party. They think he has gone home to bed.

Scene 6—Romeo sees Juliet talking to herself on her balcony. He climbs up onto her balcony, and he and Juliet exchange vows of love and talk about marriage.

EXTENSION ACTIVITIES

ROMEO AND JULIET FIGHT BACK

Shakespeare probably wouldn't approve, but let's give the young lovers a break! Have students write what they would do if they were Romeo and Juliet to convince their families to end their feud. They can write a letter, play, TV commercial, poem, or even a message for skywriting! Anything to get their parents to approve of their relationship. Encourage students to find nonviolent solutions to their problem.

THE GREAT DEBATE

Discuss with students how they think the feud between the Capulets and Montagues got started. Something very bad must have happened for these families to hold a grudge for so long. Ask students if they have ever argued with someone and then forgot how the argument began. Have them share their experiences. Then invite volunteers to participate in a debate. Choose two teams of four or five students—one team can be the Montagues, the other, the Capulets. Have one team debate why the feud should end, the other why it should continue, keeping in mind the time period. They can also debate as to when and how the feud began. Invite the rest of the class to decide on a winner.

CHARACTER REPORT CARDS

On a graphic organizer, design a "report card" for students to "grade" characters from the play. Include possible grades (A–F), a "Comments" section, and a list of qualities to be graded (e.g., *Prejudiced, Loving, Kind, Violent, Dependable, Rash,* and *Uses Common Sense*). Divide the class into small groups, and assign each group two or three characters from the play to "grade" according to the qualities listed on their report cards. For example, Romeo might receive an "A" for *rash*, but how will he be graded on *common sense?* Groups must discuss their grades until they come to a consensus. Have students list reasons for their choices in the "Comments" section. As an extension, invite students to find quotes in the play on which to base their grades.

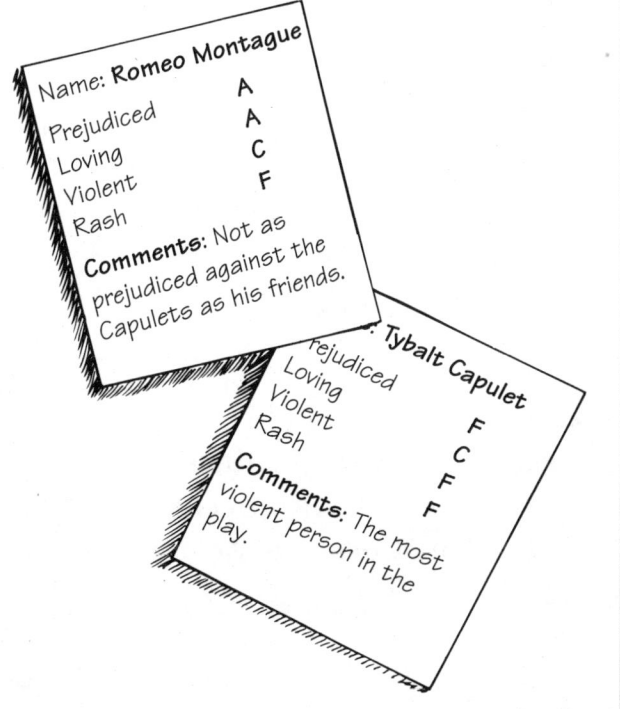

© 1997 Good Apple

EXTENSION ACTIVITIES

ROMEO AND JULIET THEME SONG

Invite student pairs to each find a song with lyrics relating to the themes of the play. Students will need to define the song's theme and relate it to an aspect of the play. Have students write the lyrics on a transparency and bring in a tape of their song to play for the class. You may want to assign students specific acts or scenes to ensure a variety of music and themes (and cut down on the love songs). Keep the tapes to play as background music or during the intermission of the play's production.

ADVICE COLUMN

Read and discuss some typical advice columns from the newspaper. Then invite each student to choose a character from the play for which to write a letter. Have students think about their characters' problems and write letters (in first person) to request advice. Collect the letters and distribute them to different students. Now acting as wise advice-givers, have students write letters of advice to the characters. You may want to do this activity before reading each act of the play, so students can see if their advice was followed in the following act. Discuss which characters gave advice in the play. Was it good advice? Was the advice followed? What were the results of following or not following the advice? How would the story be different if the characters followed the advice generated by the class? As a variation, invite student respondents to write advice as another character in the play. For example, Juliet could write the nurse for advice, and the responding student would write a letter back as if it were from the nurse.

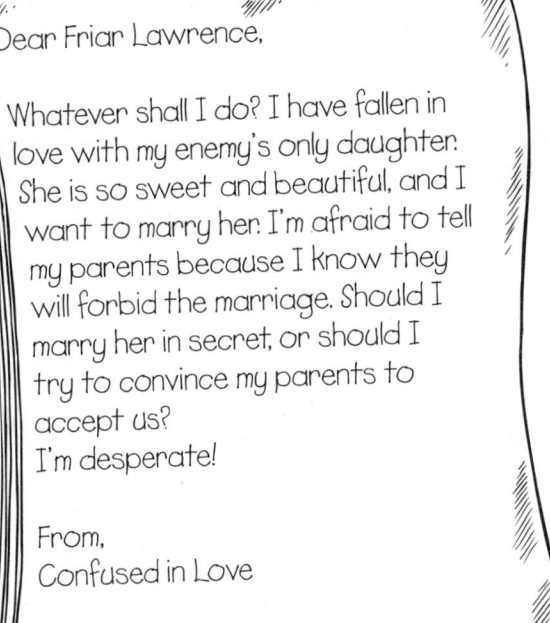

Dear Friar Lawrence,

Whatever shall I do? I have fallen in love with my enemy's only daughter. She is so sweet and beautiful, and I want to marry her. I'm afraid to tell my parents because I know they will forbid the marriage. Should I marry her in secret, or should I try to convince my parents to accept us?
I'm desperate!

From,
Confused in Love

SCENE TITLES

Have students write titles for each act and/or scene in the play. For example, Act One could be titled *Romeo and Juliet Fall in Love Amongst the Feuding*; Act One, Scene One, *The Feud Continues*; Act One, Scene Two, *Juliet Must Marry*; and Act One, Scene Three, *The Lovers Meet*.

EXTENSION ACTIVITIES

AGREE/DISAGREE

Romeo and Juliet contains many morals, lessons, and opinions about life. Invite students to think about these issues as an introduction to the play. Before reading the play, write the following statements on the board.

I believe in love at first sight.

My parents know more about love and relationships than I do.

I would be willing to die for my friend.

Sometimes it's necessary to disobey your parents.

Older people are more prejudiced than young people.

There is never a good reason to kill someone.

You shouldn't fight your friends' fights.

Have students write *Agree* or *Disagree*, responding to each statement. Ask them to add one or two sentences explaining their answers. After they finish, read each statement aloud and ask students to raise their hands to show how they voted. Discuss the issues as a class. They should generate animated and lively debates.

After you have studied the play, ask students to review each statement to see if they would change any of their answers. Then invite them to answer various questions from the perspective of characters in the play. For example, *Was it right for Juliet to marry Romeo for love rather than obey her parents' wishes and marry a man she didn't love? Was Romeo justified in killing Tybalt after Tybalt killed Romeo's best friend Mercutio?*

ROMEO AND JULIET QUARTO COVER

Shakespeare's plays were first published in quarto and folio form. A *quarto* is a small volume containing one Shakespeare play, and a *folio* contains several plays. Invite student groups to create quarto covers for *Romeo and Juliet*. On the inside front cover, have them write a brief summary of the play, mentioning both the main plot and subplots. The inside back cover should contain some information regarding Shakespeare's life and an artist's rendition of "the bard." Have students draw and color an amusing or important scene from the play for the front, including the title, author, imaginary publishing company, and price. Then have students write one-line reviews for the back cover, for example, "An exciting, yet tragic story of forbidden love. I couldn't put it down!" "A page-turner from beginning to end!" Display student work on a bulletin board or for guests to review at your performance.

EXTENSION ACTIVITIES

PLAY POSTER AND TRAILER

Have student groups each create a poster depicting the themes of the play. They can choose a quote from the play as a headline or make up one of their own, and write copy describing the main events or highlights. Invite students to paint or draw original pictures and/or use magazine cutouts to show symbols representing the play's main ideas. These posters can be used to advertise your upcoming production.

Students can also make a trailer for the play. (A trailer is a short preview containing highlights from the feature play or movie.) Trailers should only last about three minutes, so encourage students to highlight only the most intriguing quotes, climactic moments, and tender scenes. Review several movie trailers found on movie rentals to give students an idea of what constitutes a typical trailer. Assign each part of the production to a different group (e.g., videotaping, acting, writing the narrative for the voice over, directing, and so on). At the end of the trailer, have students include the names of the actors, director, writer, and others involved in the production. Make the trailer as an independent activity or tie it into your production of *Romeo and Juliet* by using the actual actors and actresses from the play and showing it as a preview to the actual performance.

ROMEO AND JULIET TOGETHER!

Invite students to write a different ending to the play so that Friar Laurence's plan works out for Romeo and Juliet. Have each student write a summary of a new final scene, including what would happen next in Romeo's and Juliet's life together. Would they have children? Would they move away or stay in Verona? Would their families stop feuding because of the marriage?

EXTENSION ACTIVITIES

ROMEO AND JULIET REVIEW

Show students several examples of newspaper movie reviews and discuss the style in which they are written. Then invite students to write reviews of the play following these directions.

1. Attach a real (or drawn) picture of yourself to a piece of paper, and write your name, grade, and school.

2. Begin your review with one descriptive word such as *boring, exciting,* or *funny.* Write a brief review of the play, including supporting reasons why you chose that particular word.

3. Explain what you believe to be the best and worst aspects of the play.

4. Choose a character you like and one you dislike. Give reasons for your choices and how these characters affected you.

5. Give the play a grade such as: A—*Outstanding,* B—*Good,* C—*Okay,* D—*A bomb!*

CHARACTER SCRAPBOOK

Have students, individually or in groups, make a scrapbook for one of the play's characters. They can include letters from other characters, keepsakes from the masque, pictures or drawings, ticket stubs to special events, love notes, awards, and so on. Encourage students to add to their characters' lives, imagining what has happened to them outside the boundaries of the play, but to not remove any actual facts or events. This activity brings depth and understanding to the characters as opposed to a flat, one-dimensional perspective. Keep scrapbooks in a central location for others to browse.

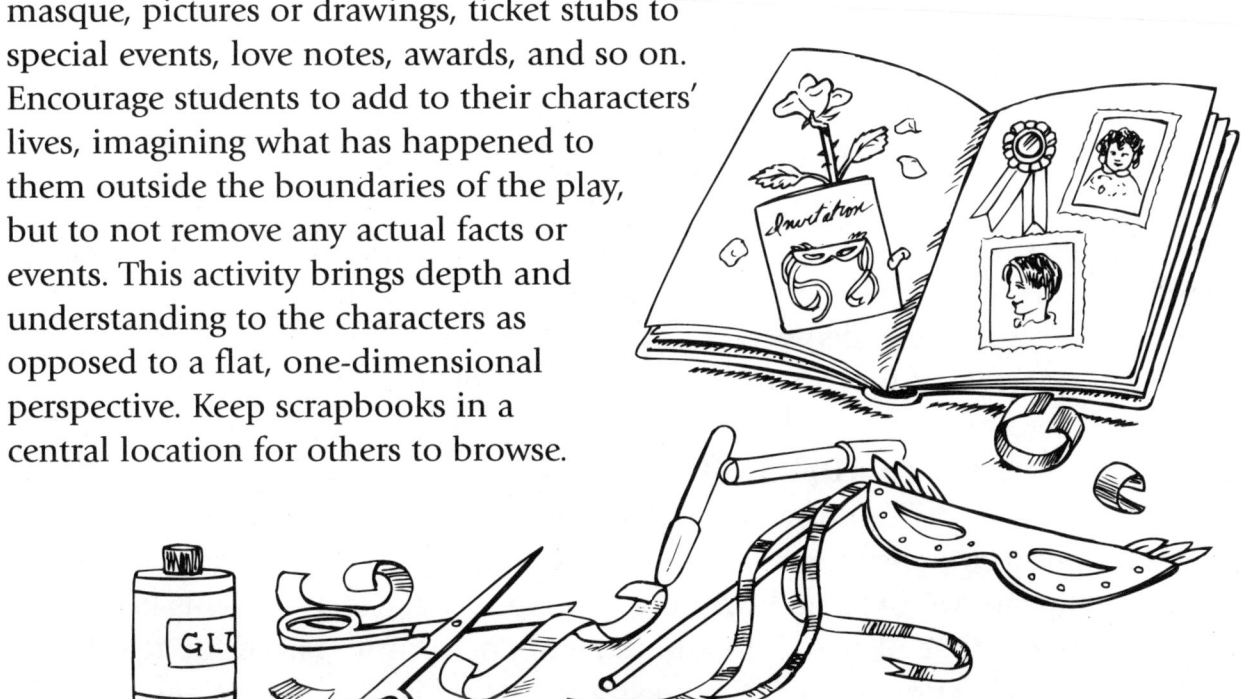

EXTENSION ACTIVITIES

REBUILDING THE GLOBE

Invite student groups to construct small versions of the Globe Theatre. They can use boxes, cardboard tubes, tagboard, fabric and wrapping-paper scraps, yarn, and various other art supplies. Make sure they refer to an accurate picture of the Globe and include the many special attributes of Shakespeare's stage, including trapdoors that fall into "hell" and a canopy above the stage as "heaven." Encourage students to be creative and add actors onstage as well as patrons in the audience. Invite students to display their creations. As an extension, invite groups to "act out" a scene from the play using their theatres, and characters made from cardboard, spools, or even sock puppets, depending on the size of the models.

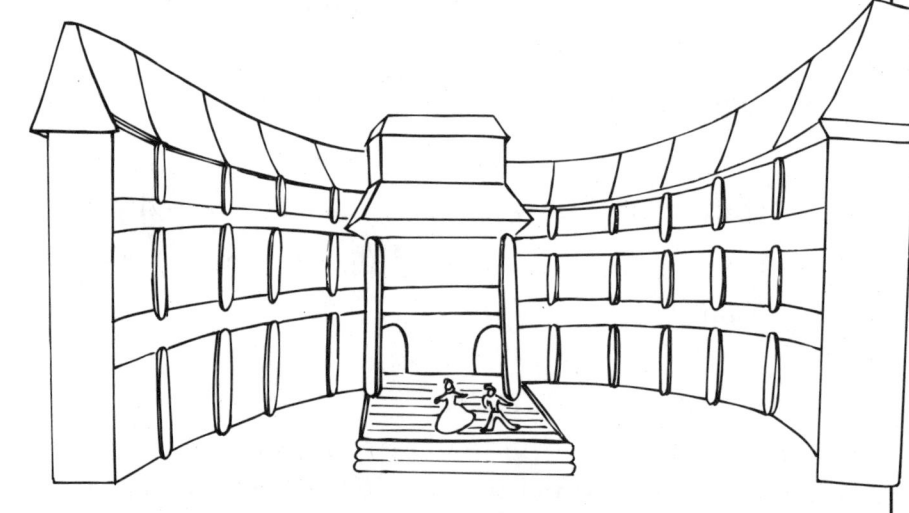

DEAR DIARY

After studying each act of the play, invite students to choose a character who appears in that act. Have each student write a diary entry from the character's perspective, describing how he or she feels and what he or she plans to do. Students will look forward to seeing what their characters actually decide to do in the following act. This helps students look into the minds of the characters, see things from their perspective, and predict what what will happen next in the story.

ALL THE WORLD'S A READERS' THEATER

You may wish to perform the play as a readers' theater rather than a full production. This technique allows students to participate with little preparation. You can even assign two or three students to one role. Make sure students have thoroughly reviewed the play and their lines before performing. Even though this will be an informal performance, encourage students to wear costumes and stand or walk around when their characters are speaking.

EXTENSION ACTIVITIES

PLAY POP-UP BOOKS

Divide the class into five groups, and have each group make a pop-up book for one act of the play. To make books, have students fold a sheet of construction paper in half and cut several "pop-out" tabs in varying lengths (see illustration). They will need one sheet for each scene. Then have them draw and cut out characters and/or props needed for each scene. Invite students to draw a background on the paper's upper half and glue characters/props to the tabs so they pop up when the page is opened. Have students choose a line they feel best represents each scene and write it on the paper's bottom half. Bind each group's pages into a book, so you have one book for each act of the play. You can also have students make only one book, with one page for each act. These books are great to show off at Back to School Night, at the play's production, or during your Renaissance Feast!

RENAISSANCE FEAST

To close your study of the play, celebrate with a Renaissance Feast! Have student groups research the time period (Elizabethan England) in which the play was written via the Internet or the library. Topics can include food, sports and games, clothing, music, housing, entertainment, and so on. Invite each group to share what they learned with the class, and use the information to plan a feast. They can dress up in period clothing, prepare special foods to eat, play games, and listen to period music. You may invite parents and/or another class to your feast so students can share what they've learned.

REFERENCES

Coxwell, Margaret J. "Shakespeare for Elementary Students," *Teaching PreK–8* 27, no. 8 (March 1997): 40–42.

Epstein, Norrie. *The Friendly Shakespeare.* New York: Viking, 1993.

The Illustrated Stratford Shakespeare. London: Chancellor Press, 1982.

Lipson, Greta Barclay, Ed.D. and Susan Solomon Lipson, M.A.T. *Romeo and Juliet Plainspoken.* Parsippany: Good Apple, Inc., 1985.

Onions, C. T. *A Shakespeare Glossary.* New York: Oxford University Press, 1986.